Jason,

Over the years often spoken issues and concerns affecting higher education. The opportunity to share my thoughts on this book was a welcomed opportunity. I hope that you will find them of some help as you move through your career in higher education —

Love Dad 4/16/08

Latino Change Agents in Higher Education

Latino Change Agents in Higher Education

Shaping a System That Works for All

Leonard A. Valverde
and Associates

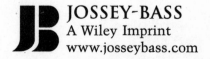

JOSSEY-BASS
A Wiley Imprint
www.josseybass.com

Published by Jossey-Bass
A Wiley Imprint
989 Market Street, San Francisco, CA 94103-1741—www.josseybass.com

Jossey-Bass books and products are available through most bookstores. To contact Jossey-Bass directly call our Customer Care Department within the U.S. at 800-956-7739, outside the U.S. at 317-572-3986, or fax 317-572-4002.

Jossey-Bass also publishes its books in a variety of electronic formats. Some content that appears in print may not be available in electronic books.

Library of Congress Cataloging-in-Publication Data

Latino change agents in higher education : shaping a system that works for all / Leonard A. Valverde and associates.—1st ed.
    p. cm.—(The Jossey-Bass higher and adult education series)
  Includes bibliographical references and index.
  ISBN-13: 978-0-7879-9595-9 (cloth)
 1. Hispanic Americans—Education (Higher) 2. Latin Americans—Education (Higher)—United States. 3. Educational change—United States. 4. Educational equalization—United States. I. Valverde, Leonard A.
  LC2670.6.L40 2007
  378.1'982998—dc22

                            2007029351

Printed in the United States of America
FIRST EDITION
HB Printing 10 9 8 7 6 5 4 3 2 1

The Jossey-Bass
Higher and Adult Education Series

Contents

Dedicated to
all who fought for social justice
in higher education,
particularly those who are no longer with us

Juan Aragón
Roberto Cruz
Raúl Murgia
Américo Paredes
Irma Rangel
Tomás Rivera
George I. Sánchez
Henry Trueba

Foreword

Urgency is the main theme in this collection of essays by well-respected Latino educators from various professional backgrounds in higher education. Reform of the current U.S. system of education, especially higher education—its structure, goals, curriculum, and instructional pedagogy—is desperately needed, they argue, if the country is to address the educational needs of Hispanics. Failure to do so will have dire consequences for the United States, they predict, and will ultimately jeopardize its standing as a world power in an increasingly competitive and knowledge-based global economy that is highly dependent on skills in mathematics, science, and technology.

The authors argue forcefully, supported by data from multiple sources, that drastic changes are essential in order for Latinos, currently the largest minority group and projected to become 25 percent of the total U.S. population by mid-century, to be educated at rates comparable to those of the majority, and thus be able to contribute their knowledge and skills, including their English-Spanish bilingualism, to the nation's economy and in fostering improved relations with our Latin American neighbors. Failure to realize this on the part of the nation's leaders and policy makers will condemn future generations of Americans to significantly lessened levels of economic prosperity.

To support their claims and arguments, the authors provide readers with data documenting the rapid demographic growth of the U.S. Latino population over the past few decades. Although the majority of Latinos are still concentrated in a handful of states, their numbers have spread to other regions of the country, including several cities in the South that now have sizable—and fast growing—Hispanic populations. The growing economic clout of Hispanics in the U.S. economy, where in 2005 their purchasing power exceeded $650 billion, is projected to reach a trillion dollars by the end of this decade.

These realities stand in stark contrast to the dismal statistics presented throughout the book of the nation's educational system which show extremely low rates of academic attainment at all levels for Latinos. The seemingly intractable problem of Latino school drop-outs is highlighted, along with the lower participation rates in higher education, where most Latinos who manage to attend college enroll in two-year colleges and often do not graduate or successfully transfer to a four-year institution. In spite of special programs created to assist Latinos and other underrepresented students to prepare, enroll, persist, and graduate from middle school, high school, and college (such as the various federal TRIO Programs, GEAR UP, Title V—Hispanic-Serving Institutions, and ENLACE), as well as programs such as Mathematics, Engineering, Science Achievement (MESA), designed to address the even greater underrepresentation of Latinos in the so-called STEM disciplines (science, technology, engineering, and mathematics), Latinos still lag significantly behind their peers. Six-year college graduation rates are very low, and even lower in graduate and professional programs.

A focus on some states where Hispanics constitute a large percentage of the population, such as California and Texas, reveals that their enrollment in higher education is severely limited. The reasons behind this unfortunate state of affairs are multiple: urban and rural public elementary and secondary schools that provide students with an inadequate academic preparation, attributable in many cases to serious underfunding; inexperienced teachers; few counselors; overcrowding due to inadequate facilities; and a lack of instructional equipment, such as computers. As colleges and universities compete for the best students by offering merit-based (in contrast to need-based) scholarships, students from families with limited financial means find themselves struggling against difficult odds. Latinos who manage to enter higher education— typically the first in their families to attend college—often find themselves facing rising tuition and fees, limited or reduced grants with a concomitant reliance on loans to finance their education, and few networks of cultural or academic support on campus. As a result, many leave without completing their degrees or transferring to a four-year campus. The number of Latino faculty members in public colleges and universities in California and Texas is also relatively small and, as figures provided in the book show, their percentages have increased only slightly over the past two decades. The same holds true for Latino administrators, although some gains have been registered among those who serve as academic support and nonfaculty staff.

Under these conditions, one might expect that the authors would express great frustration and anger at the slow pace of change in academia. But that is not the case. Instead, the tone of many of these essays is one of patient, cautious optimism about the future. While acknowledging the limited success that has been achieved by U.S. colleges, as evidenced by an increasing number of Latinos who have obtained baccalaureate or graduate degrees, and who have become successful professionals and joined the nation's middle and upper socioeconomic classes, the authors also recognize the sad, frustrating reality of the many who are left behind every year. As leaders, they are committed to their success, too. Having grown up in environments similar to those of many of these students, and having not only survived but also achieved success in academia, several authors share poignant narratives of their own evolution as students and the turning points in their careers that led them to where they now find themselves, serving as advocates of students in similar circumstances. Their personal testimonies and reflections address the conditions facing Hispanics as they struggle to gain a foothold in our educational system. More important, they also point to specific action steps that can be taken to change this unacceptable state of affairs. Instead of calling for the development of a new plan to address the current crisis, they prefer to send a clear signal that things will not be dealt with in a "business-as-usual" manner by calling for a new Grito Fuerte, a direct reference to El Grito de Dolores, the 1810 declaration by Father Miguel Hidalgo y Costilla that marked the start of Mexico's struggle for independence from Spain. This call to action, issued to higher education leaders and policy makers in general, is amply supported by compelling evidence found throughout the book.

This volume also represents a call for leadership. The authors remind those who hold leadership positions at all levels—especially Latinos—that they must take courageous action, even in the face of difficult circumstances, in order to bring about concrete, positive results. For example, to the leaders of institutions defined in federal legislation as "Hispanic-Serving Institutions" because 25 percent of their students are Latinos, the suggestion is made that, as a measure of public accountability to the Hispanic community (and for the country as a whole), the federal Title V legislation should be changed so that preference would be given to institutions that not only enroll but also graduate significant numbers of Hispanic students, accurately labeling them as "Hispanic-Graduating Institutions."

Regarding students, it is generally recognized that avenues of leadership are often open to the graduates of elite institutions of higher education—private as well as public flagships—based on their reputation and on the networks that can be developed in them by students and graduates. That is why so many parents try so hard to get their children into certain types of institutions. However,

Latino students do not apply in large numbers to these colleges, and many students and parents who are uninformed consider all university degrees to be of equal value. The authors encourage Latino students and their parents to explore all of the options open to them in higher education, including elite institutions—Ivy League colleges, private four-year liberal arts colleges, and flagship state universities. Many of these institutions have significant funding for scholarships and need-based grants, and they represent important avenues of opportunity for Latinos and other underrepresented students in higher education as many of the United State's future leaders will emerge from them.

In no way is this suggested course of action meant to diminish the vital role of the overwhelming majority of public and private two-year and four-year colleges, where the bulk of U.S. higher education students, including Latinos, will continue to enroll and be well served, and from which the majority of the nation's college graduates will come. It simply highlights an important potential resource that high-achieving Latino students should seriously consider as they weigh college choices.

It was indeed fortunate that the authors in this volume devoted themselves to a period of intensive dialogue and collective reflection over two days, for out of their pláticas emerged a distillation of their thoughts, followed by their individual, analytical, and well-informed commentaries which draw on their significant experience in higher education. Our country's leaders and policy makers would do well to heed their advice.

Ricardo R. Fernández
Lehman College–CUNY
Bronx, New York

Preface

The focus of this book is the future of the United States. It is written to help individuals, institutions, and communities to be creative, independent, strong, resourceful, and vibrant. More specifically, the targeted benefactors are Latinos[1] in the United States, but much of the proposed efforts found in the text will benefit other persons and communities of color, such as African Americans, Asian Americans, and Native Americans, as well as low socioeconomic Whites. Its primary purpose is to recommend changes in our institutions of higher education so that Latinos and other traditionally underrepresented racial and ethnic groups can be educated to their fullest potentials. As a result, American society and in turn the Western hemisphere will benefit economically and socially. Some of my colleagues with a longer calendar and more expansive thinking than I would raise the stakes to include the world by the end of this century as well.

Since 1980, demographers, economists, labor leaders, and politicians, among others, have been pronouncing "the decade of the Hispanic." Demographers may have coined the phrase when they calculated the rapid increase of the U.S. Latino population. Economists made their own declaration when they

[1]In this book the term *Latino* includes male and female. Also the terms *Hispanic* and *Latino* will denote Raza (race) and will encompass all of the various subgroups: Mexican American or Chicano, Cuban, Puerto Rican, and Central and South American.

discovered the impact of the Latino as a significant consumer. Labor leaders captured the phrase when they became aware of the growing Hispanic workforce across the country. Political parties used the phrase when they wanted to increase party membership and voter turn-out for their candidates. By 2005, similar predictions were being made, but instead of using the "decade of the Hispanic," newspaper accounts began substituting "century of the Hispanic." This word change began with the 2000 Census; it was predicted that Latinos would become the majority by 2050 in the high-growth states of California, Texas, New York, Florida, and Illinois. This may occur closer to 2025, if the Latino population continues to grow faster than predicted. The *Arizona Republic* newspaper had a report with the headline "1 in 2 new Americans since 2000 is Hispanic: U.S. adds 12 million residents; 6 million are Latinos" (Kamman, 2005). The article reported: "Since 2000, the Latino population has expanded nearly three times faster than the nation as a whole. Hispanics now constitute 14.1 percent of the nation's population estimated at 293.7 million. That's an increase from 12.5 percent in 2000 and 9 percent in 1990."

Besides the explosion in population numbers, another change has emerged. Latinos are now living all across the United States. Whereas in the past, Mexican Americans lived primarily in the Southwest and Midwest, they now live in "traditional" southern states, like Georgia and South Carolina. Puerto Ricans and Cubans no longer limit themselves to the Northeast and Southeast respectively. They, too, are moving westward in greater numbers than in the past. Lastly, more Central and South Americans who are migrating to the United States now live in the eastern metropolitan areas of Boston, Chicago, New York, Philadelphia, and Washington, D.C., besides the usual western cities of Los Angeles, Denver, Albuquerque, San Antonio, and Kansas City.

What does the growth of the Latino population in the United States mean for society in general and higher education institutions in particular? Change—transformational change and systemic change! Since the 1950s with the beginning of the Civil Rights movement, efforts have been made to provide equal opportunity and social inclusion to groups previously discriminated against based on their skin color. In education, this translated into equal educational opportunity, and in the higher education arena, it has meant greater access and better retention. However, most higher education and social institutions in the United States took the shallow approach of admitting but not trying to fully incorporate these constituents into public agencies and new students into colleges. In this approach, nothing major was wrong with the public schools, colleges, and universities; instead the Latino and other minority students just needed to meet the standards, apply themselves, make the necessary social and educational adjustments, and all would be well. After all, the system had supposedly worked for other immigrant groups in the past. Under this segregated type of thinking, the general strategy adopted by institutions of higher education was to find "soft" external money to start a program that would target a specific population and provide tailored support services. These specially seed-funded programs were add-ons and did not replace existing outdated programs or change the institution. Even when these special programs proved to be successful in helping targeted students gain admission and maintain a satisfactory academic status, the institution continued to give priority to its traditional programs over the add-on programs. When a budget decision had to be made as to which would be sustained, the traditional program was favored over the minority-focused program. These new special populations programs had to find their own means to sustain themselves or they would die due to lack of institutional resources.

The real value of this book is that the views expressed herein are not what a person would likely hear at open discussions on campuses among staff members. The point of reference taken by the chapter authors is what is best and needed for Latinos, not the institution. Their perspectives have been formulated from years of firsthand involvement and observation. The chapters in this book represent significant points made at a discussion held in Austin, Texas, in February 2005 when the Hispanic Border Leadership Institute (HBLI) convened a *platica*, the Spanish word for conversation, of more than thirty seasoned scholars and academic leaders. (If their years of service were added together, the collected total would be well over 750 years of experience!) In order to capture the tone and passion of the large group discussion, we asked contributing authors to write in the first person as much as possible. The Austin Platica was a two-day gathering to examine the past forty years and discuss how much progress or regression had taken place in the Latino experience in postsecondary education. We were not just trying to ascertain the advancements made but also lessons learned as to why Latino success was so limited. As the forum continued and we interacted and shared our observations, we collectively concluded what most of us had individually come to understand. We needed a grand design and all-encompassing plan for Latinos in higher education. If we were going to be successful in reversing the minimally productive efforts of forty years of hard labor, the nation must respond with systemic organizational change. And so the discussion turned to posting a new manifesto, quickly referred to as El Grito. This book is written by individuals who throughout their careers have worked to change educational institutions and organizations so that a new majority of students of color could benefit commensurately. Educational institutions would become better able to serve students and richer in value for undergoing comprehensive change. Hence the title of this book, *Latino Change Agents in Higher Education: Shaping a System That Works for All.*

This is not a niche book, narrowly targeted to one population, and therefore, limited in value. Higher education leaders are coming to the same conclusion that most Latino academic leaders are: Higher education must redirect, redefine, and restructure itself in order to become more inclusive, and most important, open to promoting diversity. For example, *Taking the Reins* (Eckel & Kezar, 2003), sponsored by the American Council on Education (ACE), recounts the cases of twenty-three universities that are attempting to transform themselves. These institutional change cases were supported by the W.K. Kellogg Foundation. Another example is an independent effort initiated by Michael Crow upon his appointment as the new president of Arizona State University. His goal is to make over ASU into a "new American University." Outside the university community, economic and business leaders are calling for higher education institutions to reform themselves on a major scale. In June 2005, the Committee for Economic Development, a nonpartisan business policy group, released a report called "Cracks in the Education Pipeline: A Business Leader's Guide to Higher Education Reform." While there are many good specific recommendations made in the report, it gives the overall impression that existing leadership within institutions of higher education is resistant to change. Higher education needs imaginative leaders who can go counter to conventional thinking. Time and circumstances have changed, so too must leadership approaches change with these parallel societal changes. For this reason, many of the chapters emphasize leadership.

Let me end by emphasizing one last point. For too long, the voices of our Latino scholars and academic leaders have gone unheard or, when we have been forceful about expressing our ideas, they have been ignored or dismissed. Our interpretation of reality is different than the mainstream's because we have been kept on the margins. With changing demographics, the development of technology, and the formation of a global economy, those in the minority are now becoming the majority. Our perspective needs to be not only heard but acted upon. Thirty years ago, when I was just starting my career in higher education, I interviewed Dr. Juan Aragon, an established Latino scholar and academic leader, then president of New Mexico Highlands University, to gain as much early and helpful insight as possible. Learning the history and surveying the landscape was one of the keys I was taught when in training to be a change agent. After a full-day interview and numerous ideas shared, one lasting lesson I learned from my interview with Dr. Aragon was what he called the "power of definition." Those persons in a position to define the problem, typically policy makers and institutional administrators, would be in power to determine the solution accordingly. These elected officials and selected chief executive officers would shape, if not dictate, reality to conform to their definition.

This book is just one of those moments in time where we are defining the future, not just for Latinos, but for all.

Leonard A. Valverde
Executive Director
Hispanic Border Leadership Institute

Acknowledgments

I wish to express my appreciation to the many persons who helped in the making of this book. First, I wish to thank all the participants who attended the Austin, Texas, Platica in February 2005, where the idea for this book germinated. In particular I wish to thank Michael Mulnix who, as the editor of the *Journal of Hispanic Higher Education*, urged me as the convener of the Platica and director of the Hispanic Border Leadership Institute that sponsored the Platica to edit a book that represented the perspectives expressed at the conference and encouraged some of the participants to be contributing authors. Second, I wish to thank all the contributing authors who accepted my invitation to write a chapter. I realize this was a hardship for them since most had major administrative responsibilities to attend to daily. Third, I wish to thank Sandy Chavez Lopez, my administrative associate, who helped greatly in the formatting and revising of the manuscript. Fourth, I wish to thank those individuals whose counsel I sought in the writing of this book, specifically, Baltazar Acevedo, David Ballesteros, Roberto Haro, and Monte Perez.

About the Contributors

Silas H. Abrego is the associate vice president for student affairs at California State University-Fullerton. He earned his doctorate in higher education from the University of Southern California. Dr. Abrego has worked throughout his career to enrich the educational experience and quality of services for students. He has been a visionary leader in the planning and implementation of highly successful outreach and retention programs and leads efforts to provide scholarships and educational enhancement programming for low-income and first-generation college students.

Baltazar Arispe y Acevedo Jr. is the director of the center for applied research at the University of Texas-Pan American and professor of educational administration. He has over thirty-seven years of experience at all levels of education in both the public and private sectors. His research has been in the areas of public policy, institutional advancement, demographics, diversity, organizational development, workforce and economic development, as well as issues directed toward disenfranchised communities.

Ed Apodaca is vice president for student services and enrollment management at the University of Houston-Downtown Campus. He has been in higher education for over thirty-five years in the fields of student services and enrollment management at the University of Houston, the University of California-Riverside, University of California-Santa Barbara, University of California

Office of the President, University of Massachusetts-Amherst, and San Francisco State University.

David Ballesteros is dean emeritus and professor of Spanish and cross-cultural education at San Diego State University and visiting professor of organizational behavior at Universidad del Azuay in Cuenca, Ecuador. His professional career spans forty years in education as a high school teacher, community college instructor, university professor, dean, and vice chancellor for academic affairs. His publications include topics in language teaching, bilingual-bicultural education, community-based education, and teacher preparation.

Manuel N. Gomez is vice chancellor of student affairs at the University of California-Irvine. He is nationally recognized for his creative and innovative work in the development of educational partnerships to advance access to higher education for minority students. He is also a published poet.

Roberto Haro, a Mexican American scholar and activist, is a retired professor and university executive with career service at the University of California, San Francisco State University, State University of New York, the University of Maryland, and the University of Southern California. His doctorate is in higher education administration and public policy. Haro taught ethnic studies and was assistant chancellor at the University of California-Berkeley and headed the team that planned and developed the new California State University at Monterey Bay. He retired in 1999.

Henry T. Ingle is vice chancellor for instruction, planning, and technology with the San Diego Community College system. He has anchored a variety of educational development programs in the areas of new information technology, distance education, and online instruction for the University of Texas at El Paso. He earned his doctorate from Stanford University.

Yolanda R. Ingle is the assistant vice president for institutional advancement in the areas of alumni relations, fundraising, and corporate and foundation cultivation work at the University of San Diego. Prior to this appointment in 2006, she held the same position at the University of Texas at El Paso. She received her doctorate from the Claremont Graduate University in California.

Gloria Ann Lopez is dean of arts and sciences at Del Mar College in Corpus Christi, Texas. She earned her doctorate from the University of Texas at Austin; she has completed postdoctoral education at Texas A&M University and Harvard University. Dr. Lopez served as director of instructional programs in the Community and Technical Colleges Division of the Texas Higher Education Coordinating Board and also served as dean of continuing education at Eastern New Mexico University-Roswell. She is currently president of the National Council of Instructional Administrators.

Monte E. Perez is vice president of student services at Golden West College. He earned his doctorate in public administration and public policy from the University of Southern California. Over his lengthy career, he has served in a variety of roles. He has been the assistant director of admissions at Stanford University, the director of the Educational Opportunity Program and Student Support Services at California State University-Los Angeles, a policy analyst for the U.S. Department of Education, and director of the Educational Testing Service's western regional office. Lastly, while at the National Hispanic University in San Jose, California, he was the director of institutional research and the vice president and provost of academic affairs.

Leonard A. Valverde is the executive director of the Hispanic Border Leadership Institute and professor of higher education at Arizona State University. Throughout his forty years in education he has been a vice president for academic affairs in Texas, dean of the fifth largest college of education in the nation, and a department chair. He started as a classroom teacher in the Los Angeles City public schools and was promoted to an area supervisor of math teachers. He has been elected president of the Texas Association of Chicanos in Higher Education and the chair of the Hispanic Caucus of the American Association for Higher Education. His goal has been to champion the improvement of education for all students of color and Latinos in particular.

Latino Change Agents in Higher Education

Part I

The Past Cannot
Be the Future

Part One provides sound reasons why it is not only in the best interest of the United States to make a paradigm shift in its delivery of education to Latinos, it is also necessary if we are to remain a global power. The chapters in Part One share a view that the scope of change in higher education is much broader and deeper than just helping Latinos. Current special efforts are inadequate since society and demographics are changing, and higher education is struggling to serve white students as well. Institutional change goes beyond the boundaries of four-year universities to K–12 schools and societal enterprises as well.

We open in Chapter One with the major arguments as to why the higher education community, in conjunction with governmental bodies and other significant agencies and organizations, needs to transform itself in order to provide greater access, create institutionwide holding power, and produce successfully educated Latino students. The major reasons for systemic change in institutions of higher education are to: (1) complete the social justice agenda, (2) embrace changing demographics, (3) strengthen the national economy, (4) advance higher education institutional viability, (5) reshape local communities, and (6) lead the way to forming a global society.

Chapter Two provides some initial reflections on reengineering higher education institutions in terms of technology and resources so as to meet not just the educational needs of Latinos, but their life needs as well. Husband and wife coauthors Henry and Yolanda Ingle share a view that even though society has been globally transformed, the higher education community is stuck in an outdated dysfunctional mindset. Their view is representative of other higher education Latino change agents. They suggest a number of conceptual pathways that should be put in place so that the exponentially growing new student demography is better prepared to contribute and shape the culturally diverse, globally interdependent society. They put forth a set of new models that are evolving to better match the learning needs of students and recommendations on how better to capture much-needed private resources (both from Latinos and non-Hispanics) for public institutions to be more successful with all students of color.

Chapter Three widens the focus of how to improve the education of Latinos to include the K–12 public school system and noneducation groups. Gloria Ann Lopez reminds the reader that the poor conditions of schools serving Latino communities have been created by state politics, and these same politics have been applied to institutions of higher education serving Latino communities. Lopez argues that since the disconnected systems of K–12 schools, community colleges, and four-year universities have worked against a quality education for Latinos in the past, the three levels must collaborate as an "all-in-one-system" in the future. While the illustrations come from Texas, the lessons learned and dynamics observed are applicable across the country.

Why the United States Can No Longer Wait to Educate Its Latino Population

Leonard A. Valverde, Baltazar Arispe y Acevedo Jr., and Monte E. Perez

Plain and simple, by 2050 if not sooner, the future of the United States, now in an information age, could be in the hands and, more important, in the minds of its Latino population, which numbers 44.3 million as of 2007 (Arizona Republic, 2007). The current White majority of the United States must become a vested stakeholder in a sustainable agenda that results in preparing Latinos to assume leadership roles in this country's economic and social development. The only remaining question is: Will the traditional restrictive power brokers in the United States surrender the educational infrastructure and allow it to be transformed to better educate Latinos? By systematically changing public education, the United States will be able to prepare its Latino sons and daughters to enter into leadership roles and in so doing keep the United States competitive in the global economy and socially conscious to eradicate discrimination and promote democracy around the world. If the United States wants to safeguard its future, then leadership development through a college education will have to be available to the ever-increasing numbers of Latinos, the lead group in the new ethnic majority. This chapter presents six compelling reasons why higher education in the United States must begin now to provide greater access and opportunity for success for future generations of Latino students. The six imperatives for U.S. institutions of higher education to act on are: (1) complete the social justice agenda, (2) embrace changing demographics, (3) strengthen the economy, (4) advance higher education institutional viability, (5) reshape local communities, and (6) lead the way to forming a global society.

The above statement of Latino influence and importance in the future development of the United States should not be taken by the reader as overly grandiose. It may seem so given that reported history has omitted many of the contributions of Latinos in the United States. But like their African American brothers and sisters, Latinos both as individuals and as a group, against great odds, have established an impressive record of achievements in many arenas. Latinos have been instrumental in establishing southwestern agriculture, particularly in California, ranching in Texas, and mining in Arizona (McWilliams, 1968). They have provided leadership in public office such as former governor of Arizona Raul Castro, Senator Joseph Montoya of New Mexico, former Denver mayor Frederico Pena, and HUD Secretary Henry Cisneros under President Clinton. They have served in the military; during World War II, Mexican Americans received more Congressional Medals of Honor than any other ethnic or racial group (Morin, 1966). They have made advances in sports (Roberto Clemente), in music (Tito Puente), in education (George I. Sanchez), in the legal profession, and as inventors. In short, as the heightened public debate rages on about illegal immigration, the general public should remember that the United States was built by the work and hard labor of its immigrants. Just as it can be said that Black slavery made cotton king in the United States, so too did Mexican labor make agriculture king.

The United States can no longer underserve its neglected and oftentimes abused Brown population. The following six imperatives lay the foundation for the remaining chapters in the book, that is, why higher education professionals and elected policy makers should pursue this book's recommendations.

Social Justice

If the United States is going to be stronger in the future, it must heal itself from the social illness of discrimination. This social affliction emerged before the birth of this nation with slavery (called the "peculiar institution"), and throughout the nation's lifetime has become epidemic in proportion. People of color refer to America's racism as a cancer because over time it has spread and been deadly for far too many persons. Discrimination continues to negatively affect the U.S. workforce, making it weaker and less productive; and its leadership, which remains biased against certain groups, thus leaving human resources untapped. If this type of social illness continues without some form of treatment, the U.S. economy, legal system, and government will stagnate. If discrimination is allowed to continue, the United States is in danger of falling behind other countries economically, politically, and socially. An undereducated and underprepared minority population will soon become the majority, opening the door for countries such as China and India to become world dominant.

Latinos, along with other minority groups, are already the majority in some states, such as California, and within certain metropolitan public school districts such as in Los Angeles, San Jose, and San Diego. Along with California, New York, Illinois, Florida, and Texas are high-growth states, and each has a Latino majority in most of their urban school districts. Simply put, Latinos and other new racial/ethnic majorities are the future workforce, consumers, and leaders of this country. So what needs to be done? Latinos must be prepared through a quality K–16 education to assume leadership roles in society and to enter professions that historically have been denied to them. We must end wrongful practices that produce exclusion. We must eliminate denial of opportunity. We must stop unfair treatment. To halt these discriminatory and exclusionary behaviors, we must remove their sources and change the belief that denial of civil rights does not hurt the nation at large.

Discrimination is not acceptable, and to continue to act in such prejudicial ways in the future will not only harm the group discriminated against, but the entire United States. History has been cyclical. In the 1760s, the American colonies engaged in the slave trade. In the 1860s, the country found itself in a civil war, in part over slavery. In the 1960s, riots over civil rights broke out. As the Kerner Commission Report (Kerner & Lindsay, 1968) then concluded: "We have two societies, one white and one black; one rich and one poor, separate and unequal" (p. 1). Will the United States find itself in a similar situation in 2060 or sooner over institutional exclusionary practices of persons of color? Abraham Lincoln said it best when campaigning to become president, "This country can not endure being half slave and half free." By 2050 (and probably sooner), the U.S. Census Bureau predicts the Latino population will be the majority in certain states like Texas. If the United States does not excise its racism, particularly in its public institutions, then the United States may experience another set of civil disorders to overcome exclusion, end White privilege, and have true equal opportunity.

In 1970, Thomas P. Carter, in one of the earliest treatments of the subject, *Mexican Americans in School: A History of Educational Neglect*, made the observation that because many Mexican Americans hang on to substantial elements of their Mexican culture, they as a group continue to occupy low social status. He went on to pose the question, why has the school failed to offer Mexican Americans substantial aid toward climbing the social ladder? In this book, the writers are addressing similar issues within the context of higher education institutions and their governance structures as well as the overall economic framework that is continuously evolving as we shift more to a global, technologically grounded economy. Nearly forty years after Carter's inquiry, the challenges are basically the same; Latino communities across the nation are not progressing socially commensurate with their population growth. Equally, institutions of higher education are not adding value to the Latino higher education experience. Under these circumstances, how can the United States maintain its place as a world leader particularly in higher education? The answer is it cannot.

Changing Demographics

When a population increases in a democracy, it should translate into greater influence by way of representation and bridge the gap from exclusion to full participation. The demographic data about Latinos as reported by the U.S. Census 2000 Count create many favorable expectations and promising results such as more political power through representation, expanded educational opportunities, more funding for local communities, greater economic leverage, and more participatory social roles. According to the 2000 Census, Hispanics are the youngest and fastest growing demographic. In 2000, Latinos were 13.5 percent of the total population, and by 2005 they were 14.2 percent. By the year 2018, Hispanic students are expected to account for 29 percent of public high school graduates. White students, who represented 62 percent in 2002, will go down to 45 percent. Hispanics currently make up 15 percent or 4.1 million of the total traditional college-age population of eighteen- to twenty-four-year-olds in America. By 2020 they will comprise 22 percent of that population (Santiago, 2005). In California, the Latino population is projected to grow by 33 percent during the ten-year span of 2005 to 2015 and upward of 30 percent from 2015 to 2025 (U.S. Census Bureau, 2004). In Texas, another major Hispanic demographic state, by 2023, three out of every four Texas workers will be non-Anglo (Murdock, 2005). These demographic shifts are not just in California or Texas but also pronounced in New Mexico, Arizona, and Colorado.

Nowhere is this Hispanic growth more evident than in the 2004 public school enrollments in major southwestern urban centers: Denver (57 percent Hispanic student enrollment), El

Paso (79 percent), San Diego (42 percent), and Albuquerque (55 percent) (WICHE, 2005; Baran, 2005; Texas Education Agency, 2005).

Latinos, once concentrated in certain regions, are now spread throughout the nation, although the greatest concentration is in the southwestern states (see Tables 1.1 and 1.2).

While the Hispanic population is dramatically increasing, there are not corresponding increases in graduation rates, higher education enrollments, economic participation, and other such indices.

Table 1.1. Ten States with the Largest Latino Population by Region

Region		2005 Population	% of Total U.S. Latino Population
Southwest (5)		23,819,114	61[1]
	California	12,534,628	33
	Texas	7,882,254	20
	Arizona	1,679,116	4
	Colorado	895,176	2
	New Mexico	827,940	2
East (3)		7,771,967	20
	Florida	3,433,355	8.5
	New York	3,026,286	8.5
	New Jersey	1,312,326	3
Middle States (1)			
	Illinois	1,807,908	4
South (1)			
	Georgia	625,382	.01

Sources: Chapa & De La Rosa (2004) and Pew Hispanic Center (2006b).

[1]While the Southwest region has 61% of the U.S. Latino population, the East and Middle states regions are included (even though incomplete) to show comparison.

Table 1.2.   Twenty-Two States with More Than 100 Percent Increase in Latino Population by Region

Region	Percentage Increase in Latino Population 1990–2000[1]	2000 Latino Population	2005 Latino Population[2]
Southeast (2)			
N. Carolina	394	378,963	544,470
S. Carolina	212	95,076	136,616
South (5)			
Georgia	300	435,227	625,382
Tennessee	278	123,838	171,890
Alabama	208	75,830	98,624
Kentucky	172	59,939	65,179
Mississippi	147	39,569	
Central (6)			
Arkansas	337	86,866	130,328
Nebraska	155	94,425	124,504
Iowa	153	82,473	102,047
Oklahoma	108	179,304	218,987
S. Dakota	108	10,903	
Kansas	101	188,252	218,244
Middle States (3)			
Minnesota	166	143,382	185,464
Indiana	117	214,536	273,004
Wisconsin	107	192,921	230,715
East (2)			
Delaware	136	32,277	50,007
Virginia	105	329,540	440,988
Northwest (2)			
Oregon	144	275,314	360,000
Washington	106	441,509	546,209

(continued overleaf)

Table 1.2.   *(continued)*

Region	Percentage Increase in Latino Population 1990–2000[1]	2000 Latino Population	2005 Latino Population[2]
West (2)			
Nevada	217	393,970	557,370
Utah	138	201,559	264,010

Sources: Chapa & De La Rosa (2004) and Pew Hispanic Center (2006a).

[1] Increase is from 1990 to 2000 Census count.

[2] 2005 population figures from Pew Hispanic Center (2006b).

In Texas, while 39.35 percent of all public school students are eligible for the free school meal program, which is based on poverty guidelines that are established by the U.S. Department of Agriculture, data show that 90 percent of all students in the Lower Rio Grande Valley school districts (which is made up of 95 percent Latino) are eligible in this same free meal program. A 56.65 point difference between the entire state of Texas population and Latinos in South Texas reveals the large and growing discrepancy in the status of poverty within Texas and what Latinos receive in state services (DeLuna-Castro & Kluver, 2005). In California, Hispanics received lower amounts of financial aid when compared to all ethnic groups in 2003–2004 and were less likely to take college preparatory courses required for freshmen admissions in California's higher education institutions (Santiago, 2005).

While college enrollment has been increasing in increments, only 20 percent of college-age Hispanics were enrolled in college compared to 41 percent of Whites, 31 percent of African Americans, and 60 percent of Asian/Pacific Islanders (U.S. Census Bureau, 2002). A higher percentage of Hispanic college students (51 percent) are enrolled part-time compared to White (40 percent), African American (43 percent), or Asian/Pacific Islander students (40 percent) (National Center for Education Statistics, 2002). The majority of college-going Hispanics are enrolled in two-year institutions (58 percent) while the other ethnic cohorts are enrolled at a less than 50 percent rate in these same institutions. A report issued by the Education Trust (2006) states that major research and land-grant institutions are falling behind in enrolling students of color with the exception of Asians.

In terms of outcomes, Latinos have increased their graduate enrollment but are still underrepresented in proportion to their population. In 2000, Hispanics comprised a lowly 5 percent of all graduate students, while Whites comprised 68 percent, African Americans 9 percent, and Asian/Pacific Islanders 5 percent. Hispanic women now have a higher percentage of enrollments in both undergraduate and graduate programs where they represent a minimum of 60 percent of the total (National Center for Education Statistics, 2002). Hispanics are earning more doctorates, but the number is still relatively small. In 2001, they earned only 3 percent (1,440) of these 48,000 degrees, while Whites earned 61 percent, African Americans earned 5 percent, and Asian/Pacific Islanders earned 6 percent (National Center for Education Statistics, 2002).

A report by the American Council on Education (2006) reveals that minority enrollment in higher education across the country grew between 1993 and 2003. However, the proportion of Hispanics was still not as high as that of White students. Further, and more revealing, the report concluded that the increase of Hispanic students in higher education can be credited to overall population growth and not institutional efforts.

Economic Vitality

The Latino population is increasing, but their educational outcomes, particularly college admission and graduation rates, are out of proportion to these dramatic demographic shifts and this, in turn, negatively affects their participation in the economy and their political participation. In order for the United States to remain an economic giant, it will have to take at least two actions with regard to the growing Latino workforce. First, it will have to upgrade its public educational system, from kindergarten to graduate school, so that the majority of Latinos are better educated. Second, the U.S. business community will need to attract and retain talented Latino youth.

Jobs in the United States for people with associate degrees are projected to increase by 26 percent or 1.3 million by 2012 and for those with bachelor's degrees by 20 percent or 3.6 million, both surpassing the overall U.S. job growth rate (Mingle, Chaloux, & Birks, 2005). In the future, a college-educated person with an advanced degree will be the staple of a high technology, global economy. Major U.S. corporations having to compete worldwide will be seeking well-educated, highly skilled individuals, who can work in a multicultural world.

By 2020 in California, a high-growth state, it is expected that half of its entire workforce will be of Hispanic origin (Public Policy Institute of California, 2005). Besides the U.S. business community actively recruiting a better-educated workforce, companies in Central and South America, Europe, and Australia will be seeking U.S.-educated workers. Latinos, because of their bicultural experience, will be highly sought after employees.

But the economic picture is not just one of production, the rendering of services, marketing, and sales; it is also buying, consuming, replenishing, and use of services. In short, an economy is only as strong as its consumption base. As the Latino population increases, they become a larger market of consumers. As of 2006, Latinos have more than $700 billion in purchasing power, and that figure is expected to top the one trillion dollar mark by 2008 (United States Hispanic Chamber of Commerce, n.d.). For example, this is particularly evident in the purchasing of Hispanic food products and financial services. With many large, multigenerational families, Latino households spend an average of 46 percent more per week on groceries than the general public. In financial services, enterprises that handle money transfers to Latin America are growth industries. More than 30 billion dollars a year flows from the United States to Latin America (J. Friedman, 2005).

Yet, even with Hispanic growth in the labor force and its ever-increasing purchasing power, the United States remains vulnerable to global competition because Hispanics continue to remain in the lower rungs of the educational ladder. More than half of Hispanics do not have a high school diploma and only 10 percent obtain a bachelor's degree (U.S. Department of Education, 2004). This lack of education limits the ability of the Hispanic population to contribute to the nation's economy as consumers and as taxpayers. The United States' social security fund may only be available to the tidal wave of retired baby boomers if the United States' future Latino workforce can contribute sufficiently.

If the future U.S. workforce is only as good as its preparation, then education in the United States will have to change. Not only change, but be transformed. Why? It is well documented that Latinos are doing poorly in K–12 schools. Secondly, because there is a dysfunctional K–16 educational continuum, admission into colleges and universities is too low as a result of poor K–12 instruction. And even those Latinos who do enter into higher education find a difficult environment, and as a consequence less than half complete an undergraduate degree.

Institutional Vitality

An overwhelming majority of Latinos fail in schools at all levels. In fact, as Latinos proceed up the grade levels, the fewer persist, and the higher the grade level, the further behind in achievement Latinos fall. The national average reported drop-out rate for Latinos has been as high as 44 percent (Valverde, 2002). It is probably higher given that state departments of education are known for skewed definitions and incomplete reporting. The 2005 National Assessment of Educational Progress report shows that eighth-grade Hispanics scored 27 points lower in math than their White counterparts, and fourth-grade Hispanics scored 20 points lower in reading than White students (Valverde, 2006). The drop-out rates keep getting worse, and the achievement gap has remained steady. Schools have done either a poor job of educating Latino youth, particularly those whose English language is limited, or done a good job of preparing Latino youth for unskilled, low-paying jobs, and as a consequence kept them from going to college.

Higher education can no longer depend on a large White freshman class as in the past. Higher education can no longer allow more than half of its Latino enrollment to be unsuccessful in earning a bachelor's degree. Higher education can no longer depend on grants from the federal government and other external sources to create and operate specialized programs that recruit or support students of color. Nor can higher education allow the successful staff members of these effective special programs to leave when nonuniversity funds run out.

As indicated by K–12 enrollments and projections, White student enrollment is decreasing and student of color enrollments are increasing. Hispanic students had the greatest increase in the rate of high school completion over a ten-year period (1993–2003), with 7.8 percent growth, compared to a 2 percent growth for Whites (American Council on Education, 2006). Therefore, the future majority of students in colleges and universities will be students of color. The only scenario where White students can continue to be the majority in postsecondary institutions is if universities deliberately cut down their enrollments by half or more. Obviously, this downsizing scenario is not viable. However, higher education institutions do tend to be in denial. A report by the Education Trust (2006) found that land grant institutions in particular are increasingly interested in attending to "older" (code for White) students.

If students of color will be the new majority on campuses across the country, then colleges and universities will have to transform themselves, adopt new paradigms, and reverse the minimal progress of Latino students. In the 1960s, higher education institutions were forced to open their doors via affirmative action litigation, primarily to African American students. Since then, the higher education agenda has been primarily concerned with access, but starting in the 1980s retention was added to the agenda. However, both these agenda items were perceived as tangential; the minority student groups were on the margin, and therefore the campuses did not need to change their mainstream operation. If these students were a small minority of the student body, the institution could continue to operate as it always had in the past.

Only recently have major professional associations (such as the American Council on Education) and higher education scholars begun to propose that postsecondary education has to change substantially across the board—its curricula, faculty and staff composition, student services, and so on (see Eckel & Kezar, 2003). A few institutions are attempting to reinvent themselves, such as Arizona State University's initiative to become the New American University.

Higher education will need to partner with K–12 education, forming K–16 consortium, and treat education as all one system (Hodgkinson, 1985). Articulation, recruitment, and matriculation from middle school through community colleges to graduate school must be tighter (see Chapter Five). The core required curriculum for freshmen and sophomores must be more expansive and inclusive of various ethnic groups, and deliver instruction using the latest technology (see Chapters Two and Four). Student services need to be more culturally relevant to ethnic student groups, and higher education institutions must partner with Latino organizations to serve the Latino communities better (see Chapters Six and Nine). Faculty and administration need to represent the ethnic composition of the United States. Traditionally White postsecondary institutions can learn lessons from historically Black institutions and from fledgling institutions like the National Hispanic University in San Jose, California (see Chapter Seven).

The leadership of these institutions must redirect themselves to transform campuses. Institutional budgets must underwrite heretofore specialized programs (see Chapters Eleven and Twelve).

Reshaping Local Latino Communities

The foundation of any nation is its smallest unit, its townships or local communities. So it is the case in the United States. If the United States is to remain a world leader, then it must make certain that Latinos are prepared and that their communities are sufficiently bolstered to enrich their lives. Regrettably, this is the not the current case with Latinos in the United States. Latino communities are segregated into barrios with low property values and a high number of rental units. Within these communities, adults are employed in low-income jobs, and children attend poorly funded K–12 public schools with high drop-out rates and low participation in postsecondary education. A high percentage of Latino men are in prisons and serve in the military. Although these barrios are either a part of a larger city or county, they are governed mostly by non-Latino elected officials. As such, Latino communities have low social status. Their residents have limited opportunities for advancement, and under the current political system, they are underrepresented and their needs are typically not attended to in either a timely or sufficient way. Communities trapped in these circumstances do not inspire hope for a better and stronger United States. America cannot stand by and allow such communities to continue, especially if this is its future population and workforce majority.

A 2004 report by the Hispanic Association on Corporate Responsibility shows the dismal state of our overall community in the mainstream economy and how it is treated by the philanthropic community. Despite its demographic growth, the Hispanic community still faces substantial barriers. The top 100 U.S. money managers control 83 percent of U.S. tax-exempt assets while only

.5 percent of these assets are managed by Hispanic-owned firms. Less than two percent of corporate directors are Hispanics and less than one percent are identified as executive officers. Moreover, Hispanics comprise 10.7 percent of the private sector workforce yet are less than 5 percent of all officials and managers. Many companies and industries do not yet track Hispanic consumer performance or Hispanic vendor usage. Less than 2 percent of foundation dollars are targeted specifically to the Hispanic community and that trend has held steady for fifteen years. (Hispanic Association on Corporate Responsibility, 2004, p. 1).

Essentially, the Hispanic community is a consumer in the amount of $650 billion per year, yet has an undereducated labor pool with a majority of its workforce working at minimum wage in lower tier support jobs with no benefits and where they can be replaced by other less educated eager workers on a daily basis. Again, this present status cannot and must not continue in the future.

Local communities that have a strong core of leaders strengthen the state and nation. Leadership skills are typically gained through higher education. Therefore, institutions of higher education will need to be more aggressive in working with public schools so that the majority of Latino youth apply and are admitted to colleges and universities. Once admitted, Latino youth should be well represented, not just in the social sciences and humanities, but in the hard sciences as well. And their understanding, upon entering into college as freshman, should be that they will continue on, seeking a graduate degree. The premise here is that a college-educated person will gain a greater sense of civic responsibility and, coupled with the Latino cultural attitude of giving back in order to help others, will produce responsive community leaders.

Community leaders encourage civic engagement, and civic engagement builds community and enhances the quality of life. By harnessing this collective brainpower and effort, organized and sustained infrastructure is put into place. The product is the building of rich environments, vibrant climates, and robust atmospheres. This is the stuff that reshapes communities for the better, improves the lives of all, and makes for a promising future.

In the minds of most people in the United States, there is no leadership found in Brown communities. Not true. Civic leadership is alive and well in our current disenfranchised communities. However, since voting districts have been gerrymandered so that Latinos do not win many of the important elected offices, our civic engagement has been forced to manifest itself in the development of community-based organizations (CBOs), community development corporations (CDCs), or nongovernmental organizations (NGOs) which increase the participation of underrepresented communities by initiating grassroots efforts, like crime prevention; providing much-needed services, like after-school programs; and increasing involvement in community governance, like voter registration drives. The U.S. political process must permit more Latino leaders to redirect their energies in such roles as city mayors and state governors, so as to enable persons like Antonio Villaraigosa, mayor of Los Angeles, and Bill Richardson, governor of New Mexico, to assume mainstream leadership roles.

Hispanics as Global Citizens

Historically Latinos have been involved in an economic framework that was based on agriculture and the manufacturing of products. With the invention of the microchip, the context of the world's economy has changed forever (Gilder, 1989). In an era of high technology, knowledge becomes all powerful. As Gilder states, "Today, the ascendant nations and corporations are masters not of land and material resources but of ideas and technologies" (p. 20). Latinos will have to be prepared to assume roles in a world economy that is driven by an ever-changing information technology. In the future, Latinos will not be fighting for space on a production line but for a seat in a white collar office, where the computer is the principle tool to access facts, data, and knowledge on the Internet.

The challenge, then, for the leadership of the United States is to fast-forward its educational and social agenda to meet a series of corresponding and concurrent economic and political agendas. The first is to concentrate on the continued development of a viable educated community at all tiers of education; second, to surround those students that are already enrolled in postsecondary institutions with every means to ensure their success so that they may be competitive in a global technological economy; third, to assume more active civic engagement roles; and finally, to maintain a sustainable agenda which is directed at the continuing development of local communities as vibrant and vital components of the United States.

Data have demonstrated that the education in the Hispanic community is fragmented and dysfunctional. There is no consistent policy nexus at either the national or state levels to respond to a population that will be the economic backbone of this nation starting within the next twenty to forty years. When one looks at the present scenario, one may see a levee which is constructed of weak materials and which has many cracks and leaks. Hispanic students and other students of color are leaving or being pushed out of public schools with an incomplete education and an uncertain future. The challenge then is to develop proactive educational policies and programs that are directed toward success which are measurable and accountability based. Slogans and catchphrases such as "Closing the Gaps" and "No Child Left Behind" simply will not do. Our Latino leadership must step forward and demand a future for Latino communities that is not rooted in an outdated economic model of the last century. The industrial model did not help our communities to advance. A technology model without well-educated Latinos will not help the United States remain a world power.

Our nation's challenge has been recognized by many such as Thomas L. Friedman (2005) who asserts that the emerging world economy will be ruled by those individuals that collaborate in order to compete globally. Another similar perspective is provided by Richard Florida (2005) who views the core of this challenge as, "No longer will economic might amass in countries according to their natural resources, manufacturing excellence, military dominance, or even scientific and technological prowess. Today, the terms of competition revolve around a central axis: a nation's ability to mobilize, attract, and retain human creative talent" (p. 3).

Hispanic educational leaders should not be advocating for educational reforms that would garner us access and policy influence over a system that is not geared to prepare our young population for a world that will be in constant technological evolution. If Latino leaders continue working to get only the larger share of revenues from federal and state agencies that are directed toward "jobs" rather than "careers," then the game is lost for us and our nation. Instead we should insist that all educational legislation and corresponding fiscal mark-ups state unequivocally that all K–12 and postsecondary students be immersed in a technologically based curriculum that prepares them to compete for high-level employment positions in the global marketplace. People employed in minimum-wage jobs with no benefits are not going to sustain the United States in the global economy.

Summary

As dire as the past has been for U.S. Latinos, the future can be very promising. There is an ever-growing Latino middle-class community and an emerging professional cadre. There is great potential and a bright future for both Latinos and the United States. The United States with Latinos as a dominant workforce and in leadership roles can redirect the United States to assist Central and South America. The majority of U.S. Latinos are bicultural and a sizeable number are bilingual. As such they can establish relationships with these countries and create an economy that will serve the entire Western hemisphere and the world. Just as the labor of our ancestors made the United States a world power, the future brain power of Latinos can bring about a new and better world. But to start this path toward the future, higher education will have to transform itself to better prepare tomorrow's Latinos. This book is aimed at opening the door to this new future.

2

Pathways to a Better Future

Reconfiguring the Educational Context for Change

Henry T. Ingle and Yolanda R. Ingle

Echoing the dramatic changes in the nation's Hispanic population that has grown to total well over 44.3 million, Jon Garrido, a Hispanic community leader in Arizona's Valley region, was heard to exclaim to reporters at the *Arizona Republic:* "Now we are everywhere" (Kamman, 2006).

His statement refers to the growing presence of individuals in the United States who trace their ancestry to Mexico, Latin America, and other Spanish-speaking regions of the world and who continue to grow as the nation's largest minority group. Many experts project that by the year 2020 a significant portion of the American population—about 70 million—will be Hispanic and more widely distributed across the country geographically. The dramatic growth of this relatively youthful segment of the American population (as of 2004 the median age is 26.9 years versus 40 for the non-Hispanic White Anglo Saxon population [U.S. Census Bureau, 2005]) is putting unexpected pressures on all societal agencies and institutions, and in particular on public schools, colleges, and universities, to rethink the way they handle their core business and how to better serve a population which historically has been poorly served by most education providers. Our educational institutions must begin to offer an array of instructional opportunities to raise the educational achievement and the economic viability of the nation and Hispanic communities across the country. In a recent film profiling the Los Angeles region, A *Day Without a Mexican*, all economic activity comes to a standstill when the Latino labor force virtually disappears. The storyline could also apply to higher education, which would also suffer dire consequences without Latino students. Latino student populations are likely to be one of the most important segments of the U. S. population, and as a result, a group that will affect the future of higher education, both from an economic and instructional perspective.

In this chapter, we, husband and wife, both of Hispanic ancestry and long-time leaders in the higher education community, share our collective forty years of experience and expertise to argue for a new business agenda in American higher education that will serve the diverse student population. We present a series of recommendations to guide and shape this new future, which will be determined by three major forces that higher education traditionally has handled with limited and piecemeal success: First, new digital media and Internet telecommunications technologies will play an important role in alternative and continuing education delivery systems and will enable higher education to respond to the challenges of student access, retention, and graduation rates. These technologies also offer "any time, any place" education for this new student demography in need of educational and continuing lifelong learning services. Second, individuals will need to master living and working effectively in a culturally diverse, globally interdependent society. This requires educators to better integrate this global context in what, how, and to whom they teach, coupled with making available very specific "just-in-time" knowledge and information important to lifelong learning, specialized socioeconomic and workforce development, and the evolving new world order. Third, colleges and universities must move away from traditional institutional development funding patterns and fiscal resource generation strategies and find new ways to support instructional innovation for a student demography that has been cast as "difficult-to-educate." As a result, higher education has both knowingly and unknowingly popularized a mindset of "blaming the victim" for low levels of minority student retention and graduation rates.

We, as do many of our Latino colleagues, argue for more creative thinking that can address the volatile and uncertain fiscal future higher education is facing both in terms of the need for flexible, creative leadership and the articulation of "success expectations" for the new student demography. It is extremely difficult for us to visualize "a day in the life" of higher education without Latinos, but we must change the institutional mindset of *los porbrecitos* (the poor little ones) that has been so injurious to Latino student success.

The Agenda for Change

Modernization and change, and indeed a complete overhaul, is the answer to the quagmire facing higher education. Higher education must focus more pointedly on the difficult dialogue that for too long has been avoided among educators and policy makers in terms of what's working, what's not, and why. If higher education is going to be successful in garnering support and resources for significant change efforts, it will have to implement institutional practices that better meet the needs of this new student demographic. This includes such things as greater use of faculty team-teaching approaches; working with more culturally responsive pedagogy; and dramatically altering the time, place, and conditions for scheduling classes so that they are more student-centered. New instructional methods are needed that can effectively integrate the new technologies and communication media to connect home, school, and work into a seamless set of venues for teaching and learning. By so doing, new teaching and learning methods can better complement the complex lifestyles of the new student demography that may include holding a full-time job, going to school, being married and raising a family, caring for elderly parents, and being responsible members of their communities.

This agenda for change should not necessarily translate into the old "brick and mortar" thinking of more buildings, more staffing, and more parking, but rather carefully thought-out alternatives for strategic transactional change targeted to altering the often dysfunctional operational culture of our institutions. Rather than just offering stepping stones or islands of innovation, institutions will need to move in a more agile manner from the pilot stage of innovative practices to more widespread adoption of these new practices across the entire institution and rapidly introduce and then sustain programs that can genuinely change the way of doing things. The strategy can no longer be making minor changes in some areas of our operations or the adoption of paste-on functions or parallel services that are eliminated during lean budget periods. Illustrative of this change is the introduction and use of online and blended course delivery that students are now validating with increasing enrollment patterns.

Institutions of higher education need to put aside the stereotyped perspective that the new student demography, and in particular Latinos, are underprepared for rigorous college curricula and that they are not motivated to work in a disciplined manner to master learning and the use of the latest technological tools for communication, knowledge exchange, and work. Within such institutional mindsets, it is often perceived that distributed learning approaches tied to the use of new information media will not work as well for Latinos and that instead, face-to-face instruction is better. However, Latino students are succeeding exceptionally well in online and distributed learning and other alternative instructional delivery systems at a number of campuses such as the University of Texas at El Paso, at San Antonio, at Brownsville, and Pan American; Miami Dade College; and Universidad Autonoma de Ciudad Juarez, Mexico. The attrition and drop-rate in these settings is reduced when the instruction is delivered in a culturally relevant manner and makes optimum use of interactive, collaborative, and attention-engaging features. Further, most Hispanic students participating in online instruction feel that they all get a front-row seat in the online modality since there are no back rows in chat rooms or lower expectations for the electronic delivery of their assignments or obstacles to voicing their ideas and perspectives. Indeed, student diversity is dramatically alive and functioning well in online teaching and learning environments where often the full continuum of the new student demography comes into play—age, gender, socioeconomic status, work experiences, and positive and negative opinions. Still, were this not enough of a justification for the use of new information media and technology in this context, students in the online modality are acquiring skills important to professional success, such as collaborative team work, using the Internet to retrieve and evaluate information, and working at a distance with others (Hispanic Educational Telecommunications Systems, 2005).

New Models for Higher Education Success

New models are emerging which indicate that colleges and universities will need major revamping to become more "user friendly" to the changing student demography. Models such as Michael Crow's "New American University" at Arizona State University and the "virtual learning marketplace" initiatives of the Hispanic Association of Colleges and Universities (HACU) strive to integrate stronger cross-cultural and global perspectives into the agenda for educational reform. This climate of innovation also is reflected across the community college sector, where the majority of Latino students in higher education are enrolled, and in the efforts of the League for Innovation in the Community College to foster technological changes in student services as well as in instruction and administration.

These new models argue for a decentralized and less "top heavy" administrative approach, or what Thomas L. Friedman in his national best seller, *The World Is Flat: A Brief History of the*

Twenty-First Century (2005), describes as more imaginative and unpredictable thinking in an increasingly flat and interconnected world. Leaders of color are realizing that higher education must leave the rhetoric at the back door and begin "walking the talk" and promoting more of a "can do" attitude in coming to grips with the challenges of the new student demography. This requires that campus culture be more student-centered, open, and experimental in its focus and less controlling with its "top heavy" management hierarchy. What is evolving, therefore, is an integrated matrix of faculty, administrative, and community-based resource teams exploring experiential learning programs, virtual working environments, and critical information exchange strategies for lifelong learning. Collectively, they can promote the change and innovation that speaks to the multifaceted challenges the new student demography faces in terms of access, retention, academic success, and graduation.

These new models require educational institutions to focus more pointedly on what is being taught, who is being taught, why and in which ways they are being taught, and indeed even where and when they are being taught. The impetus for this change in thinking is the result of changing instructional content that is now required for success in the world of work, coupled with the complex and diverse backgrounds of the learners and the unique characteristics of technology-enhanced teaching and learning. Collectively, these elements are working to link and integrate new informational resources heretofore difficult to consistently bring into the more traditional on-campus instructional settings for imparting instruction to learners. In some instances, some of the models are advancing specialized approaches for the education of different populations across different disciplines and life stages shaped by both demographic and geographical conditions. In other cases, the models are more analytical, evaluative, and synthesize learning that evolves from collaborative instructional experiences. One size, indeed, no longer fits all, and the new technology can now help educators develop different pathways to facilitate these teaching and learning challenges. There also is greater discussion about providing better linkages to enduring student learning outcomes and the "life journey" skills that an individual needs from the cradle to the grave. Beyond the content that students are exposed to in college classrooms are higher order analytical thinking, communication and information seeking skills, and critical workplace tools and abilities that over time become the enduring body of learning that students should and need to take away from a college or university experience.

Fortunately, experienced educators and administrators who reflect the demographic population shifts, such as those in attendance at the Austin, Texas, 2005 Platica symposium on education reform, are developing a better sense of the challenges of genuine educational innovation and change. We must move away from attempting to make carbon-copy higher education institutions and the "look alike" frenzy that characterizes the strategic planning and capital fundraising efforts of higher education institutions today. Otherwise, the result may well lead to what Harvard University's David J. Collis has termed the "homogenous multiversity" (Fain, 2005) or a college district that is not clear about who it is, who it needs to serve, and what it must do to remain on the cutting edge as an educational institution. Such indecisiveness can erode an institution's core strengths, institutional mission, and reference points for excellence, as well as demoralize faculty. An organizational graveyard of institutions of higher education of this nature is indeed a frightening thought.

On the financial front, the College Board and other membership associations in the higher education community have observed that our colleges and universities are fast moving away from being publicly supported to being publicly assisted. Budget resources for education have been severely cut back across all public state university and college systems where well over 60 percent of Hispanic students are enrolled. Indeed, the perspective seems to be that since a college degree dramatically increases the income potential of an individual, that person should, in turn, defray the expense of obtaining it. Thus has ensued the debate of public benefit versus individual gain in the higher education arena at a time of growing enrollment of Hispanic students with very modest means who cannot afford the mushrooming growth in the costs of tuition and fees. As Latino educators, our challenge is to inform the larger tax-paying society that one without the other, that is, either individual gain or public good, has never been an option for our community.

Ultimately, the nation benefits by valuing individual accomplishments that better our way of life. It behooves this country to better educate the Latino community, less the standard of living for the entire society be severely and negatively affected. Higher education policy analysts, such as Paul Lingenfelter and Charles Lenth, now argue that financial aid needs to become less of a form of support for higher education, and more of an instrument for ensuring that our citizens—an increasing majority who are of Latino ancestry—can compete effectively in new global market economies. This economic view, in turn, speaks favorably for Latino students who as a rule come to higher education settings equipped with both cross-cultural and bilingual capabilities that often higher education institutions do not know how to fully appreciate, nurture, and strengthen to professional levels of maturity. Many Hispanic higher education leaders observe that at this point in the United States' development as a society, the greatest and most significant sector for improvement is the development of this growing undereducated human capital. Indeed, our Hispanic population is both our greatest asset and its underdevelopment our greatest vulnerability to global competition and the future of the American way of life.

The solution lies in a postsecondary education success formula for low-income, disadvantaged students, who today constitute the fastest and largest growing segment of the population colleges and universities will need to serve well into the foreseeable future (Lingenfelter & Lenth, 2005). As a result, educational institutions truly committed to excellence in the education of all students need to focus significant time, resources, and attention to alternative instructional delivery media and methods and the development of a new pedagogy of instruction that is centered on the learning needs of this new student demography.

Planning for the Transition: Issues We Should Take Seriously

Leaders in the Latino higher education community brought together in Austin, Texas, by the Hispanic Border Leadership Institute in February 2005, collectively observed that as more change occurs, the less we will need to fear change. As fads and fashions sweep over people, professions, society, and ways of thinking, many of us are tempted to believe that this time around things will really be different. Well, those of us in the trenches of promoting and providing educational opportunities for Latinos students have been there, done that, and seen that before. Hence, we are more than jaded when it comes to expressing optimism for change and the type of resources important to this change process, but yet we are a community that believes in the future and betterment for our children. Perhaps, therefore, in this context for change, it is best to return to the "basics." This includes helping students find information, convert information into knowledge in a variety of contextual settings that they will daily confront, and in turn improve the quality of life that surrounds them. Without these basics, no one can cope with change. This change then is the challenge for the Hispanic community. That is, higher education needs to reengineer the process of both generating and imparting knowledge and critical information for change to occur in our community. This means reengineering not just for some students, but for all students, and especially for the new student demography that will form the leadership and working ranks in the American society in unparalleled numbers in the very near future.

The Issue of Resources: How Should Change Be Funded and for What Purposes

Until more recent times, public universities were funded through reliable investments of monies by respective state legislatures tied to a variety of full-time equivalents and formulae. It seemed as if the question of funding rarely surfaced as a major issue. As a result, states such as Texas and California were able to create a system of higher education unrivaled in the modern world. Nonetheless, taxpayer revolts, shifting political agendas, and a growing demand for accountability of public institutions have moved funding and related budgetary development issues to the forefront of organizational survival. In writing this chapter, we drew on our own varied postsecondary education experiences, both as Latino students at the University of Texas at El Paso (UTEP) and more recently, as administrators at this same university, charged with promoting change and innovation, and scurrying about for resources. Our experience in overcoming obstacles to shape our success of today provides a historical context for what was then, needs to be now, and will be needed in the future to facilitate many of the changes we have noted above.

During the 1960s, most of us who had the good fortune as the first generation of Latinos to attend college paid approximately $50 to $100 tuition per semester at the then public institutions like UTEP. In retrospect, these tuition rates were quite low, even when adjusted for inflation. We might add, however, that it was still a financial stretch for many of us to pay that tuition. The low tuition rates stemmed from the fact that Texas, for example, harbored a significant tax base to allocate major operational funding for public higher education institutions.

Today in Texas and other states, however, public institutions receive only 25 to 30 percent of operational and maintenance funding from the state. The reasons for the colossal drop in public funding are complex, but the result is quite clear. Public universities have had to identify other substantial funding sources to maintain their educational programs, including those that are focused on the specialized needs of the changing student demography, as well as the acquisition of new technology deemed to be essential to the business of colleges and universities.

In addition to the dramatic decline in the state's tax base, Texas and California policy makers have had to face significant changes in the demographic make-up of the population that is now seeking to be served by educational institutions. The number of Hispanics, especially among school-age Latinos, has been exponentially growing faster than most educational leaders imagined. The changes in the funding sources, both potential and real, for state institutions of higher education, therefore, have become enormous. What have these changes brought about and to what end?

Philanthropy in Higher Education: Implications for Latinos

Hispanics in the United States represent various nationalities and subgroups with cultural, racial, ethnic, linguistic, religious, and socioeconomic differences, as well as geographic localities of the country where they now reside. Because of the vast diversity in the Hispanic population, groups representing twenty-one countries, it is difficult to generalize (Wagner & Derek, 1999, p. 2). Hispanics do, however, share many values that relate to philanthropy and fundraising. According to Royce and Rodriguez (1996), several values commonly attributed to Hispanics include strong family ties, mutual respect, spirituality, fatalism, collectivism, trust, pride, dignity, respect, and congeniality. Moreover, religion has been strongly cited as the area in which most Hispanics provide philanthropic support, as reflected in the collection baskets at church services.

Historically, the philanthropic organizations have not viewed Hispanics as a significant part of the "giving" community. It is safe to say that until just recently the Latino population has been ignored by those who guide philanthropy in the United States.

There have been misconceptions that Hispanics do not have the financial capacity because of the types of jobs they have (gardeners, bus boys, mechanics, cooks, maids, waiters, and so on). The severe economic needs of Hispanics, the thinking goes, render this group unlikely prospective donors since many of their concerns still focus on day-to-day survival.

Public institutions of higher education have also paid little attention to Hispanics as donors. At the forefront of this lack of understanding, we perceive, is the fact that most public institutions of higher education have failed to inform the general pool of current students, parents, and alumni (Latino as well as other members of underrepresented groups) about the importance of giving back to their educational entities to support strategic programs that matter to all stakeholders. In essence, there has not been a conscious effort to build a "culture of giving" to higher education across the Latino community. This contrasts sharply with the private university sector. Indeed, lessons can be learned from private institutions dependent on varied sources of funding to sustain their visions and missions and who also have over the years recruited the best and the brightest of our Latino students. Early in the 1970s, major forward-thinking institutional leaders understood their responsibility in identifying and preparing individuals from ethnically diverse populations. They envisioned that by educating these individuals to serve in varied capacities within their communities and other global environments that there would be an intrinsic benefit to the U.S. society and to the rest of the world.

Public institutions, on the other hand, have been plagued by a more limited view. Within the last fifteen to twenty years, various fundraising efforts have taken precedence. Most public institutions have had to fast forward their fundraising efforts to find ways to fill the budget gaps, such as capital campaigns. In so doing, public higher education institutions targeted only the most wealthy to cultivate and engage them as alumni in order to support ongoing programs.

Recommendations

Perhaps no other area is as vital to the future of Latinos in higher education than philanthropy and institutional advancement, along with the concerns that we have voiced for new instructional methods that speak to this new multicultural reality. New models in these sectors are urgently needed to guide the efforts of those higher education institutions genuinely committed and challenged to better serve this changing student demography.

Among the ingredients needed for success are institutional advancement models tied to use of new information media and technology and the hiring of professionals in such areas as alumni relations, communications, and public affairs from the target communities that are now the norm for many successful private and public universities. Staff members work hand-in-hand with university presidents to help raise funds in order to sustain a multitude of programs not covered by state support. Still, fundraising is not the only challenge public universities face today. For the majority, the diversification of their student populations has reminded postsecondary leaders that their students have no family history that includes the college experience. Furthermore, university leaders and faculty are slowly coming to the realization that if students from diverse populations and all socioeconomic levels are not provided the opportunity to a high quality postsecondary education, then local communities, states, and even the U.S. economy will be at a risk.

Just as important is the understanding that students from a more diverse population base become stakeholders with vested interests in the public university. Until recent years, Hispanics have not been sought as donors to higher education institutions. Unlike private institutions, public institutions have not realized the benefit of drawing on a cadre of educated, economically successful Hispanic alumni who can eventually give back to meaningful causes. Furthermore, there has been a lack of interest stemming from many misconceptions held about why Hispanics give or don't give to postsecondary institutions. Hispanics have a long history of giving as long as they have a stake in the outcomes their contributions support. In many respects, we feel that institutions of higher education have marginalized Hispanics and not provided inclusive and friendly "entry points" to warrant in their own minds that that they have a stake in the institution's future.

Uppermost in our concluding reflections for reengineering higher education institutions is that they demonstrate relevance and address issues of varied communities and alumni, and if this is accomplished, they will succeed in their efforts to establish and maintain a donor base from this community. The recipe is simple if the right questions are posed and a more inviting and engaging cultural context for action is promoted.

What influences Hispanics to give? We feel Latino groups, particularly liberals, since they donate more money than conservative Latinos, need assurances that their donations will be used for causes they value, for programs that will serve Latino students well. Hispanics will participate in proposed philanthropic activities if there is a sense of belonging, of making a difference, and a sense of satisfaction based on clear indicators of accountability to achieve the desired results. The questions needing to be asked are readily apparent as are the answers to these questions.

How do we engage Hispanic communities and attract the support of non-Hispanics for causes relevant and important to Hispanics? First, we must emphasize that Hispanics realize the importance of philanthropy. Hispanics have a strong history of giving at the family, local, and church levels. Groups, such as the United Latino Fund in Los Angeles, the Hispanic Scholarship Fund, League of United Latin American Citizens, Mexican American Legal Defense and Educational Fund, and the National Council of La Raza have recognized the additional need to create structural alternatives so that Hispanics may give to broader causes as well. Public institutions of higher education also can play that role for Hispanics, but they must connect to some fundamental action strategies that the community values.

We should move from those belabored questions about whether or not Hispanics are more or less charitable than other groups. Rather, we should focus on identifying strategies for increasing both non-Latino and Latino philanthropy and higher education initiatives that are highly relevant to these donors. In higher education, there are specific methods used to identify, cultivate, and engage donors. Working with diverse donor populations has become important because of the demographic changes within institutions. Furthermore, the traditional donor pool is getting older; they have provided their share of support. Alumni involvement and engagement at an early age has emerged as an important component in fundraising. Researching the progress of alumni in their professional trajectories is relevant to all development offices as they determine the top 10 percent of the donors that will provide the major funding base for universities.

We have drawn some of these action strategies from our own career work and conversations we have held with other colleagues over the years. We think these reflections are relevant to institutions of higher education working to facilitate greater Latino participation in the quest for both relevant educational innovation, as well as in the development of strategic processes of "giving" across our community. Briefly, they include the following:

1. Make the recruitment and graduation of Hispanic students a priority of your educational institution; remember that given the shifts in demographics, these students will comprise a major part of your future donor base and the leadership ranks that you can tap for other strategic tasks.

2. Hire and support faculty and staff of Latino ancestry who are familiar with the acquisition of external resources and have the acumen to introduce innovative teaching media and

methods that support the successful completion of bachelors
and postgraduate degrees for Hispanics.

3. Strategically target individuals of Latino ancestry for mentoring and hiring fundraising professionals and developing a
culturally relevant institutional advancement agenda and
action plan.

4. Build interactive relationships with Hispanic CEOs, corporate board members, philanthropic and foundation
representatives, and other community leaders so they become
important stakeholders in attracting other Latinos to participate in your efforts.

5. Emphasize issues and programs that matter to Hispanics and
the communities they represent and at the same time market
and publicize these efforts in a forthright and genuine manner
devoid of past "smoke and mirror" public relations images.

Organized philanthropy, we feel, is realizing the need to include
Hispanics. It is no longer only about the "good ole boy networks." It
is about paying attention to those segments of the U.S. population
that are growing exponentially and need to be recognized and
valued for their long-term history of giving for several reasons.
Organizations such as the New American Alliance consisting of
successful and well-to-do Latinos are already at the forefront of this
agenda. The inclusion of Hispanics in the fundraising arena is not
only essential, but beneficial to all in the society for the near and
long-term future. It will make a strategic and significant difference
for all in the future of the country and as a result, the reengineering
of higher education. It will forthrightly and genuinely recognize
that indeed we as Hispanics "are now everywhere" and at all rungs
of the socioeconomic ladder. We are not only eager, but qualified,
to join the leadership ranks required to play a role in this major
undertaking for change. We have no other choice given the sheer
numbers of this population, their projected growth curve, and their
great need to achieve socioeconomic parity in the United States.

3

Making an All-in-One K–16 System Work

Gloria Ann Lopez

Business as usual for education is no longer a viable option. First, Hispanics became the largest minority group in the United States in the last decade of the twentieth century. According to a report by the Pew Hispanic Center, the Southeast will be most affected by the significant growth in the Hispanic population. Hispanic children are expected to make up 10 percent of students in the Southeast's public schools by 2007, which will in turn affect colleges and universities (Kochhar, Sura, & Tafoya, 2005).

Second, our Latino youth and the nation are at a crossroads. In one direction is the American economy, increasingly dependent on more schooling beyond high school. Sixty percent of tomorrow's jobs, for example, will require skills that only twenty percent of today's workers possess (Educational Testing Service, 2000; Kelly, 2005). In the other direction are new barriers to acquiring those skills, such as tuition hikes, cuts in state aid, and enrollment caps, which make it harder for Latinos and low-income students to get an education. Amidst these two colliding forces, business coalitions have been increasingly vocal in their concern that poor academic scores and lack of interest in science careers are causing the country to fall further behind in the global economy.

The educational levels of Hispanics and other students of color are in crisis. High school graduation rates for Hispanics and African Americans continue to lag behind those of White, non-Hispanic students nationally. Many of our Latino youth are ineligible for admissions into four-year universities, and far too many of those who are admitted to college must take remedial courses that don't count toward their degrees. As a result, the cost of remediation for these students continues to rise. For some, this is "too long of a road to finish" (Hebel, 2006). Access to higher education for Latino students can no longer be viewed as separate from what occurs with our youth in grades K–12. It is connected. What happens in one part of the educational pipeline has direct implications in another. Thus, colleges and universities will have to do more than just recruit as usual and not worry about retention. They will have to substantially change their philosophies of how they work with K–12 public school districts and become part of K–16 consortiums, which are emerging as strategies that work in achieving student completion goals.

Demographic Realities

With 44.3 million Hispanics in the U.S., Latinos continue to be the largest and fastest growing minority group. The headlines in a recent article in the *Arizona Republic* (Kamman, 2005) blazoned, "1 in 2 new Americans since 2000 is Hispanic," with half of the growth attributed to immigration and the other to high birthrates. Nine percent of Hispanics in the nation are under the age of five, and this population will have an enormous impact on schools, colleges, and universities in the future, particularly in border states like California, Arizona, New Mexico, and Texas but also in the Southeast (Varsalona, 2005).

The National Assessment of Educational Progress reported that while all students have improved in mathematics and science, the achievement of Hispanics in both areas lags behind their Anglo peers (Manzo & Cavanna, 2005). Fifty-three percent of Hispanic students in the eighth grade do not meet the basic levels of mathematics. By age seventeen, their math and reading skills are the same as those of thirteen-year-old White students (Schmidt, 2003). Furthermore, only eleven out of 100 Hispanics currently in kindergarten are expected to get a baccalaureate degree. These statistics have major impact on the future of this country.

Educational Outcome Issues

These alarming statistics in the K–12 grades signal poor results even after college, specifically in employment. In the summer of 2003, the Social Sciences Department Chair of Del Mar College in Texas briefed me on the results of a national search for two history positions. He reported that no racial or ethnic minorities had applied for either of the positions. Although I was a little surprised, I was not puzzled as to why.

Our failure to attract minority applicants in higher education positions is due to the many shortcomings of the public schools today. The inability to recruit well-trained K–12 teachers and the lack of funds to teach large numbers of English language learners result in high drop-out rates. The drop-out issue alone is a major challenge and an important factor in improving high school outcomes (*Time*, 2006; Hall, 2005). Aside from the personal economic impact which will face these young people who chose to leave before completion of their high school studies, there is also the negative impact on the availability of professionals for future positions in higher education, business, and other economic sectors.

The U.S. educational system is analogous to a pyramid. At the pinnacle rests the doctorate, supported by a layer of master's degrees, which are in turn supported by several layers of bachelors degrees, themselves supported by many high school graduates, and all resting on a base of K–12 students. It takes many students from every educational level to produce the next layer of students. Wherever drop-outs occur in the pyramid, whether in K–12 or college, the effects are gaping holes which weaken the layers. The number of students who successfully complete each educational layer disproportionably decreases. For Hispanics, the lack of college completion results in fewer professionals so that we cannot fill the gaps in the very professions Hispanics were once denied. As for those unsuccessful in the K–12 system, community colleges may see them again in GED programs or more likely in programs where their job options in the future are limited.

The Hispanic drop-out issue is a national and historical phenomenon seen in states where Hispanics are predominant (California, Arizona, Illinois, New Mexico, New York, Florida, and Texas). Drop-outs are common among the poor of South Phoenix and in South Texas where agriculture is critical to the rural economies, and in urban settings like East Los Angeles and San Antonio. Today's educational observers have a right to be concerned as they watch the Latino population increase but make little progress in educational success. The educational pipeline in the United States is hemorrhaging. If, in 2020, Hispanics will account for 17 percent of the U.S. population and more than half of the population in Texas in 2050, fixing the leaking pipeline requires everyone's utmost attention and collaboration (Murdock, 2004).

Recent Approaches: Reconnecting

School districts, like colleges and universities, are accustomed to working separately in curriculum development and assessment. Nevertheless, private groups, such as the Education Trust and the Bill & Melinda Gates Foundation, have guided development of initiatives helping to bring the three educational levels together—K–12, community colleges, and four-year colleges and universities. Campus Compact, K–16 partnerships and consortia, and seamless educational pipelines are frameworks which were developed in response to the leaking pipeline. Fortunately, there is precedent for a successful K–16 seamless education pipeline, an "all-in-one" system, which can provide some insights to these newer concepts.

San Antonio: A K–16 Seamless Educational Pipeline Model

In 2002, the *San Antonio Express* newspaper reported that over 50 percent of the adults in Bexar County had earned their baccalaureate degrees, confirming that most of America is now going to college ("More Residents Are Earning Degrees," 2002). In a predominantly Hispanic community, though, how did the San Antonio metroplex achieve this?

One could say that it only took 100 years of a strong private education system made-up of three Catholic K–16 pipelines to achieve this result. The history of education in San Antonio provides an excellent model of the effect of an all-in-one system. Marianist missionaries opened a school in San Antonio in 1852, welcoming children of all nationalities and religions, followed by the Sisters of Divine Providence in 1868. They founded their college, Our Lady of the Lake University (OLLU) in 1895, as did St. Mary's University (SMU). They were followed in 1881 by the Sisters of Charity of the Incarnate Word, who also established schools, later adding college courses at the University of Incarnate Word (UIW) in 1909.

The Catholic educational approach took students from early childhood through the last year of college. Their schools and colleges were recognized for their high academic standards, dedicated teachers, organized and sequenced curriculum, the smooth transitions between levels, and ongoing teacher and professional development.

Regrettably, public education in San Antonio offered no corresponding K–16 continuum. Almost thirty years after OLLU, SMU, and UIW were established, the first public junior colleges, San Antonio College (SAC) and St. Phillip's College, came into being in September 1925. In 1969 the first public university, the University of Texas at San Antonio (UTSA), was established by the Texas legislature, offering only junior- and senior-level programs. In 1983 UTSA finally became a comprehensive university.

Today, these public higher education institutions are experiencing significant growth, and their graduates are fueling the San Antonio and Bexar County economies. UTSA has a current enrollment of 17,000, and SAC has an enrollment of 23,000. Thus, through a combination of a public and private K–16 educational foundation laid down over 100 years, Bexar County was able to boast that 50 percent of its residents have bachelor's degrees.

Politics Do Matter: South Texas

Texas is a good example of what is happening nationally to Hispanics in the K–16 educational pipeline. Its history of educating Hispanic children is similar to other states. I was once told that Hispanic graduates from Texas universities went to work at the universities in the Southwest. The few individuals who had left South Texas for more education, graduated and acquired advanced degrees but were unable to find jobs in Texas universities, so they left for states where they found some acceptance.

South Texas is defined as the geographic area south of Austin, west of Houston, and to the border of Mexico. Whereas San Antonio K–16 education was mostly private, the rest of South Texas education was mostly state-supported and historically underfunded. Just as the *Brown v. Board of Education* case was about K–12 educational equity, quality, and opportunity for African Americans over fifty years ago, so were two other cases for Hispanics, *Melendez v. Westminster School District* (1946) in California and the *Rodriguez v. San Antonio Independent School District* (1973) in Texas. The 1946 Melendez case was a forerunner to the 1954 Supreme Court *Brown v. Board of Education* decision. *Rodriguez v. San Antonio Independent School District* was about "a Texas school district, 90 percent Hispanic American and 6 percent African American that was grossly under-funded compared with neighboring largely White school districts" (Bollinger, 2003–4). Rodriguez lost the school finance case, but the 1973 decision shifted the battle of public education funding to the states and all states have passed some form of public education finance reform since then (Bollinger, 2003–4).

State support of higher education was no different than that of K–12. Texas A&I University in Kingsville was the baccalaureate degree–granting institution serving all of South Texas until the late 1960s, when upper-level, four-year colleges were added to the public higher education conglomerate (Laredo, Brownsville, Corpus Christi, San Antonio, and Edinburg). Only in the 1990s, when the legislature permitted the upper-level colleges to offer master's degrees, could South Texas claim it had five comprehensive universities. This historical footnote is a significant detail in the annals of the development of a K–16 educational continuum in Texas because, when it came to graduate degrees, South Texans had access to only one doctoral program: education.

In many Southwest states where the Latino population was concentrated, education was supported by religious groups who supported education in order to propagate the faith and so taught their students to be good citizens and encouraged the adults to network and stay within their social class or business. For South Texas as other states of the Southwest, the chokehold on higher education is directly attributed to politics just as its release is.

Politics Hindering K–16 System Formation

When a powerful South Texas senator, after working tirelessly in the 1980s and early 1990s to substantially increase the funding for Texas higher education, asked for an accounting for his constituents, he was flabbergasted to learn that a miniscule of the funding would flow to South Texas universities, including the one in his own district. He learned that the state's funding formulas were based on elements which supported doctoral programs, and South Texas had no doctoral programs at the time (a lone doctorate in education would come later). A lawsuit and a series of four legislative hearings followed. I attended three of them and was surprised by the responses of well-known and respected

Hispanic community leaders in those South Texas communities to the simple query "Why did you not fight harder for more funding for colleges and universities in South Texas?" They replied that university officers would ask the Coordinating Board for doctoral programs in disciplines other than education and were told that their applications were not good enough, that there was a state mandate to strengthen the existing ones offered by the University of Texas and Texas A&M University, that there was no funding for additional doctoral and professional programs in Texas, and so, after a while, they stopped asking.

Legislators asked the South Texas Hispanic political leaders if they were aware of what was happening. A well-respected federal judge in Edinburg said they were but that the patron system would not allow them to act. A prominent medical doctor in Laredo responded that since they politically supported Governor John Connelly, and it was he who gave them the upper-level university in Laredo, they were happy to get this because no one had listened to them before.

I grew up in South Texas and was surprised to hear them blame the patron system, especially when they themselves were part of the system. In the patron system, one person makes the decision and dictates the outcome, no matter the merits of the case. While this is an extreme case, the same regrettable political model applies to other parts of the United States, only the actors and degree of influence are different.

Considering all of the graduates with master's degrees from Texas A&I University, one would expect K–12 student outcomes to be better in South Texas. However, when educational frameworks are as politically defined as they were, it is easy to see the subtle emergence of an incestuous educational system. The impact of the tight restrictions placed on South Texas universities' ability to develop and offer graduate and professional programs was devastating. South Texas Latinos who became teachers left the area to pursue other professions. Universities such as Texas A&M

University-Kingsville (TAMUK) were not encouraged to offer a doctoral program in engineering even though its engineering program had a good reputation. As a result, role models in science, mathematics, and law were rare because Hispanic students who could have passed their enthusiasm for these disciplines on to K–12 students were not encouraged or nurtured. Teachers' expectations for students have been low and the results prove it. Is it any wonder that our Hispanic students score poorly in math on state and national tests? Hispanics continue to be underrepresented in science, technology, engineering, and mathematics (STEM). According to a 2005 study released by the Commission on Professions in Science and Technology, while Hispanics have made the most progress, they remain the most underrepresented in STEM jobs. They make up 13 percent of the workforce, accounting for only 5.3 percent of all U.S. science professionals (Gilbert, 2005).

Demographics have forced educators to see the leaky educational pipeline more clearly. Flagship universities have only recently recognized that without high school graduates and transfers from community colleges (the higher education institution of forced choice for Latinos due to open admission, low cost, and location), their ability to contribute to the workforce, local communities, and research activity would be negligible. There is merit to the recent calls by groups like the Education Trust, H. Ross Perot Group, and Bill & Melinda Gates Foundation to reform the way the STEM disciplines are taught in high schools. We have increasing need to learn how to replicate San Antonio's private K–16 education system as a national public K–16 system.

Barriers to an All-In-One System

While state legislatures continue to underfund K–12 schools and higher education, creating a critical barrier to developing a seamless educational pipeline, there are other factors which are impediments, including a lack of confidence and trust between the different educational levels, marginal use of data to track students' progress, lack of opportunities which encourage teacher conversations between the educational levels, and unwillingness on the part of the educational entities to recognize societal influences in the classroom (American Institutes for Research, 2005).

Educators need to dispel the idea that only the school district, community college, or university can do particular tasks the best. For example, by continuing to spar on the quality issue, community colleges and universities perpetuate the "silo" mentality. Researchers who deplore the fact that Hispanics are concentrated in community colleges should review their statistics in light of rising cost of tuition and fees. A new study (Glenn, 2005) that compares students with similar skills and preparation shows that students who take remedial courses are more likely to finish undergraduate degrees than those with similar preparation and skills that do not take remedial classes.

Every college and university now wants to be highly ranked in college ratings such as *U.S. News & World Report* and the *Princeton Review*. For example, *Boston Magazine* columnist John Wolfson (2005) opined that colleges trying to represent the population of the United States by enrolling more people of color and more people from lower-income levels place their ratings at risk in *U.S. News & World Report*.

Increased tuition costs are making college less affordable. Even Pell grants no longer support a college education as fully as they did in the 1970s. This means that universities have to make up the difference, and they are increasingly unwilling to do so. They are much more likely to resort to recruitment of students, usually White, with higher academic credentials and students who can fully pay for their education. The consequence is that students of color and the poor are kept out of the universities and pushed into community colleges (Wolfson, 2005). Given these conditions, it is imperative that community colleges work closer with high schools and four-year institutions.

Saving for college is also an issue for Latinos because of the lack of financial resources in their backgrounds. It is a doubly tragic issue when immigration status is factored in. Stories are emerging about young children who crossed the border illegally with their parents and then entered the public school systems. They performed wonderfully, realizing the American dream until they found out they could not enter college because of their undocumented status. Some went through the whole K–12 system, gaining admissions to colleges and universities and succeeding academically only to forfeit grants because of their questionable legal status in this country. For example, *Ascribe* columnist Jennifer Wheary (2005) laments that while 600,000 of our nation's 3 million graduating high school seniors came from immigrant families, our nation does little to support their success and future educational achievement. Immigrants are expected to contribute to the nation's population by two-thirds and more than one-fourth of the labor force growth over the next decade (Wheary, 2005). We should do what was done for immigrants of another age, educate them and ensure that we have the replacements of doctors, lawyers, teachers, scientists, and informed citizens.

For some immigrant students, the cost has been too great. "They feel they belong here but are stigmatized because they lack opportunity, so states Lilienthal, an immigration lawyer at Princeton" (James, 2005). The immigration issue skyrocketed to new heights in 2006 and has caught colleges and universities off-guard. Had schools, community colleges, and universities implemented student tracking mechanisms, perhaps they would have noticed the immigration phenomenon and anticipated the need for services for these students. When a college is trying to develop its profile of success and evaluate its graduation rate, and social security numbers are used, the data can be skewed if the social security numbers are incorrect. Fortunately due to the No Child Left Behind Act, many states now track students through elementary, secondary, and higher education and will be able to generate more data on graduation and drop-out rates in the future. Some state coordinating agencies, such as the Texas Higher Education Coordinating Board, have used social security numbers to track student outcomes since the 1980s. The nation's public schools have also used tracking mechanisms using assigned individual identification numbers rather than social security numbers. This dual way of tracking is a barrier to the development of a K–16 continuum. Many states are now calling for K–16 councils where the three educational commissioners (representing K–12, community colleges, and four-year colleges and universities) form a team with business and industry. Hopefully, these councils will promote better tracking systems and in turn improve K–16 education for Latinos and other groups.

Other higher education challenges such as less financial aid, rising costs, inadequate academic advising exist, but it is imperative to point out that there are silver linings peeking through the clouds in all states. School districts, colleges, and universities are beginning to take steps to address the development of K–16 educational pipelines that work.

Collective Leadership Promotes K– 16

In the 1980s the W.K. Kellogg Foundation, through its grant-making function, embarked on initiatives to raise young people's awareness of civic engagement, encompassing volunteerism and organizational involvement (W.K. Kellogg Foundation, 2005). This was based on the thought that collectively we all work together toward a common goal, and through collective engagement emerges individual leadership. In 2002, the foundation launched the Kellogg Leadership for Community Change to promote and nurture collective and culturally appropriate leadership in communities across the country, thus the term, collective leadership.

Government and business concern for an improved educational outcome (graduates, educated and skilled workers) has been a catalyst in forcing public schools, colleges, and universities to see each other as partners. At the national level, there are organizations such as the Education Trust and the Institute of Educational Leadership which disseminate information on educational reform and strategies that work.

The Texas Coastal Bend region is an example of a community which has bonded in its quest for a K–16 seamless educational pipeline which would foster higher academic standards. K–16 program initiatives were developed which focused on the improvement of education for the South Texas area. The community was tired of being perceived as educationally deficient as the public schools became more Hispanic. The economy suffered because business and industry feared that there was no viable workforce in the geographic area and therefore decided against relocating to South Texas.

A solution was the development of the K–16 Seamless Educational Pipeline project. The project used learning communities, leveraged dollars, and began some sustainability plans for our efforts. We know that our efforts, like others across the country, are replicable. In 1998, the Texas A&M University System received a W. K. Kellogg grant to develop innovations in institutional engagement and collective leadership. Texas A&M University at Corpus Christi invited Del Mar College, my home institution, to be its team partner. With a $50,000 grant, our team was expanded to include Texas A&M University-Kingsville, and the K–16 Seamless Educational Pipeline project was born. The $50,000 grant allowed us to explore the extent of communication between the vertical education levels and to focus on the improvement of working together. We used local statistics (noncompletion rates in the Corpus Christi/South Texas area, the higher-than-state-average teen pregnancy rates, higher-than-state-average adult illiteracy rates, high drop-out rates, and low postsecondary attendance rates) as the foundation for our work and saw how these problems contributed to the stagnant economy despite the large and rapid population growth in Texas and the nation.

The $50,000 grant sustained this K–16 initiative for five years. Each year, we covered a different aspect of the educational pipeline and used the Future Search model to lead us to new findings. The Future Search model brings large groups of people together to talk about major issues. Participants discuss what is already known about the issues, identify processes that are already working, propose recommendations, and formulate goals and a plan of action.

The first year of the grant was an investigation about education in general. What were the gaps? What needed to be done to fill them? Over 150 people from the community, government, and education attended. Our evaluation indicated that more dialogue was needed. For the next four years, we focused on the available resources for education, on the meaning of the available student data in all three educational levels, on best practices, and on the future. We consulted with the Intercultural and Development Research Association (an education advocacy group based in San Antonio) because of its wealth of research on public education and with the Education Trust because of their successful initiatives with educational compacts.

We established a web site, developed public awareness advertisements, allocated funds for mini-grants, and set the stage for curriculum alignment from K–12 to college. A core group formed various task forces. Cross-institutional liaisons were formed between education and community service agencies. Other projects emerged from the K–16 Seamless Educational Pipeline activities, such as Symposium 2001, a conference for prominent educators, government, and business leaders to formulate a plan for meaningful and lasting school change, and Boys and Girls Clubs mini-grants to promote best practices. There were ongoing conversations about the local K–16 pipeline at Chambers of Commerce and their education committees and at Citizens for Educational Excellence, a nonprofit local education fund that promotes education for community development. Finally, there was an increased awareness of best practices and programs that work.

Beyond Initiatives: Sustainability

The No Child Left Behind Act raised awareness of the consequences of test score results. According to Eva Baker: "In a framework that emphasizes accountability as the path to growth, a system is demanded where responsibility for outcomes is located and rewards are assigned.... We need to know what is actually happening in classrooms, what work is assigned to students, and how teaching and learning are taking place" (Baker, 2004).

South Texas and many other states are a long way from this goal, but I can safely say that for many trying to understand test scores, the start is with curriculum alignment. Shortly after the K–16 Seamless Educational Pipeline ended in 2002, Texas A&M University System provided funds for a new initiative, the Academic Roadmap Project, a curriculum alignment project covering the four core subject areas (mathematics, science, language arts, and social studies). Area school districts, community colleges, and universities convened to identify the gaps in the curriculum in the first year, and during the second year of the project, defined goals and objectives.

When the funding ran out, a few concerned persons wanted to continue because they believed the work which had been started was important and needed closure. The college and universities continued a discussion regarding how to keep the momentum going. Then a situation arose which coalesced the above working group. A dispute arose between the Corpus Christi's mayor and the local school district's superintendent over data on the district drop-out rates which had been used to focus attention on the area's educational inadequacies for economic development purposes. The incident served to pull together individuals who had previously collaborated on the K–16 Educational Seamless Pipeline Project and the Academic Roadmap Project and resulted in the planning of a forum on the drop-out issue.

Simultaneously, four other initiatives occurred.

- The Texas A&M University System awarded a grant to a faculty member at Texas A&M University-Corpus Christi (TAMUCC) to initiate dialogue between the educational levels on the results of the Academic Road-map Project.

- Following review of Del Mar College (DMC) data indicating that 70 percent of its students were taking at least one remedial course, and the likely first remedial course was mathematics. The two area community colleges, including DMC, and the two area universities, including TAMUCC, designed a mathematics forum because several other initiatives on the improvement of the teaching of mathematics were in place.

- The president of Texas A&M University-Kingsville (TAMUK) held a summit of education leaders in the region and rather than calling for separate forums on the core subject areas, similar to the Academic Road-map Project, agreed to support the mathematics forum planned in 2005–06.

- In addition, the tenets of a National Science Foundation grant at DMC and an initiative at TAMUCC and TAMUK to assist fifth-grade teachers whose students would be taking the state's mathematics test (Texas Assessment of Knowledge and Skills or TAKS) for the first time were used to frame the discussions.

In reviewing the multiple initiatives to improve mathematics education in the Coastal Bend, it is easy to believe that collaboration leading to an all-in-one educational system is possible.

The Coastal Bend Collaborative on Mathematics convened to investigate mathematics and related issues, always with a focus on data. Sample tests from Texas Assessment of Knowledge and Skills (TAKS), Scholastic Aptitude Test (SAT), and Texas Higher Education Assessment (THEA) demonstrated that each level requires different teaching approaches.

Academic advising issues have emerged with curriculum alignment issues. Colleges, such as Austin Community College, are developing initiatives which encourage students to pursue more education. College Connections is a program which targets college juniors and seniors and high school students, and provides assistance with financial aid forms and college applications, as well as advising on college goals.

Initiatives such as these that connect high school and college are but a few examples which are nationally coalescing with the help of foundations like the Pew Charitable Trusts, the Pew Hispanic Center, and the Bill & Melinda Gates Foundation.

Early College High School

The Early College High School (ECHS) is another model which aims to reform high school education. During the past decade, the Bill & Melinda Gates Foundation has financially supported the design of small high schools (400 students) which blend high school and college classes so that students not only complete high school but take the initiative to continue on to college. They graduate with a high school diploma as well as two years of college credit. Targeted students are from low-income families and ethnic minorities. High expectations that students engage in rigorous courses of study, staff collaboration, and learning communities are some of the elements of the program. Dual credit college and high school courses are essential elements of program design.

Lessons Learned

The nation is now realizing that a K–16 educational continuum is necessary, easy to design, yet difficult to implement. Curriculum alignment is essential to the development of a successful continuum for student advancement. Following are elements of a successful K–16 partnership:

- The changes have to be top-down from the *very* top as well as bottom up.

- Changes are systemic not band-aids.

- There is political and public recognition of the problem and support for the initiative.

- Additional monies are available.

- There is a structure to sustain the initiatives.

- A structure connects all three levels and is systemic in focus as well as integrated.

- All stakeholders are involved in discussing the issues, developing strategies, and implementing solutions.

The nation cannot afford to continue doing business as usual in K–12 schools or in colleges and universities. The future demographics will be different, but the future will be dark if young Hispanics are not educated. K–16 collaboration becomes more relevant when the three educational levels—K–12, community colleges, and four-year colleges and universities—operate not separately but rather as one system.

The current disconnected K–12, community college, and four-year institutional arrangement has not served Latinos in the past. Certainly it will not serve Latinos in the future. Therefore, K–16 collaborations involving all three educational levels are mandatory.

Part II

Systemic Change, *Sí*; Special
Add-On Programs, No

This second part of the book begins with Chapter Four that demonstrates that past and current approaches to addressing the underrepresentation of groups of color has been at best minimally successful. By analyzing data in the two states (California and Texas) with the highest concentration of Latinos and the greatest population of Latinos, Apodaca shows that the piecemeal approach of special programs has had inadequate results. Institutions of higher education will need to adopt an entirely different strategy if they are serious about providing real access and being successful in educating Latinos and other underrepresented groups. Support for higher education has decreased substantially, while growth of the Latino population has exponentially increased. The new strategy must be equal to the task and promote systemic and transformational change.

Chapter Five shows that even with a superficial commitment by institutions to greater access and retention for Latinos, Latinos have been successful in designing and implementing specialized programs. Abrego discusses fundamental program components that need to be part of successful access and retention efforts. Lastly, it should be noted that many of the effective elements identified in the first and second generation of access and retention strategies came from the thinking of Latinos and other excluded populations. Hence we know the roots of the problem and have proven we can solve the problem permanently. In a subtle way, we are justifying our conclusion that band-aid approaches are no longer sufficient. Entire campus revision needs to take place, and Latinos are best to lead the revision.

In calling for institutional change, Chapter Six speaks to going outside of the institution to professional associations to create change. Higher education institutions are conservative and resist change, thus when change does occur, it is typically brought upon from the outside.

Chapter Seven takes the position that since established institutions have resisted significant change, it is now time to create an alternative higher education institution that is designed to truly fulfill the educational needs of Latinos. Perez offers ideas for delivery of instruction and new revenue streams to help states to stimulate and finance these new Hispanic-serving institutions.

4

From Minority to Majority
New Education Strategies

Ed Apodaca

In October 2006 the United States' population surpassed 300 million, and the milestone was most likely reached by a baby boy born to Mexican immigrants at a Los Angeles hospital. Latinos will soon be a driving force in the nation's economy and politics. However, their long-term influence will be determined by their educational attainments.

In the United States, an education is the single most important asset an individual can obtain to ensure personal and professional growth and to become a more productive member of the community. Latinos are the fastest growing and youngest population in the nation and face major problems acquiring the much-needed education, as institutions keep falling farther and farther behind in providing the services and support they need. In many of the nation's K–12 schools, both urban and rural, Latinos are becoming the majority group, bringing with them a wide range of educational needs that existing traditional systems are not equipped to address. As a result, their K–12 completion rates are the lowest, and to say that Latinos are experiencing a difficult time transitioning through the educational pipeline is putting it mildly. "Hemorrhaging" is a better description of the leakage that is occurring for Latino students in the K–12 system. The Intercultural Development Research Association (2006) has conducted studies which show that in Texas almost half of the Latino students who enroll in the ninth grade do not receive a high school diploma four years later. Their reports show that school districts continually submit reports that seriously undercount the drop-out rates of students, especially Latinos. Not only do most reports confirm that Latinos are less likely to complete high school, but the Latinos who graduate are usually less prepared to pursue a college education than other students.

As the state and national populations of Latinos have increased, so have their numbers in colleges and universities, which would normally indicate that Latinos are making progress. However, a review of the data shows that the increased college enrollment is a result of the rise in population and that Latinos are enrolling close to home, usually in community colleges. The majority of Latinos enrolled at four-year institutions are at the undergraduate levels and in the soft sciences. At the graduate and professional level, Latinos remain seriously underrepresented especially in math- and science-related areas. One of the long-term advantages for faculty in higher education who teach in science- or math-related fields is that they are more likely to get key academic administrative positions.

One could argue about who is at fault for the lack of Latino representation in higher education, and the blame could easily be shared among many. Even though colleges and universities have initiated special programs designed to recruit and serve underrepresented students of color, and for over forty years received funds to do so, the results are less than what is declared at the annual conferences, such as the American Council on Education or the American Association for Higher Education (when it was in existence) by speakers who direct successful programs. Such presentations obscure the need for institutional change.

Colleges and universities have avoided accountability by providing lists of accomplishments, citing programs they have in place, using anecdotal information from reports, and proclaiming annual improvements. If the numbers of students, faculty, and administrators reported by campuses reflect the national picture, then the number of Latinos and other minorities would be much greater than portrayed by these exemplary programs. Yet, Latino representation has not changed significantly, and the increases seem to reflect population growth rather than campus-initiated change. The gap in the Latino population growth rate and student enrollment remains, and on some campuses has widened. It is clear that the accomplishments and programs cited by campuses are misleading. For example, a campus could claim that the hiring of new Latino faculty was up by 50 percent but fail to mention that that number reflects an increase from two Latino faculty members to three. In addition, the gains in minority hiring are in politically safe areas, such as undergraduate recruitment, tutorial and retention efforts, or the student service areas. Rarely do institutions report gains in key academic programs, in tenured mainstream faculty positions, key administrative positions, or in academic curriculum changes.

Most institutions still have programs and efforts initiated in the 1960s and 1970s, which were considered temporary "band-aid solutions" that would be replaced with permanent structural changes. Annual reports submitted in the 1970s and the 1980s regarding accomplishments and proposed efforts designed to increase minority representation could easily be resubmitted today with minor changes, and few would notice the difference. What makes matters worse, while society has changed, these old strategies have not kept pace.

There are a growing number of colleges and universities that are now headed by Latino presidents; however most are not in research institutions that offer terminal degree programs that prepare students for top academic positions. The majority of Latino presidents are at two- or four-year institutions located in predominantly minority communities. While this is an important step toward change, especially since many are doing well, Latinos are capable of providing the same quality of leadership as white administrators currently heading traditional large public institutions.

The lack of progress comes at a time when the U.S. Census Bureau reports that Latinos are the largest minority group in the United States and that the Latino population will grow at a faster rate than any other group even into the middle of the twenty-first century (Hebel, 2006). The tremendous growth of Latinos is already apparent in the more populous states like California, Texas, and Florida, where they are replacing Whites as the majority group. The U.S. Census data show that the nation's population grew from 227 million in 1980 to 296 million in 2003, that it is getting older, and that as a result, the college-age group (ages eighteen to twenty-four) has dropped by 5.5 percent. At the same time, over a twenty year period (1980–2000), the college-age Latino population is bucking the trend with an increase of 2.8 million or 142 percent (U.S. Census Bureau, 2004).

A report by the Western Interstate Commission for Higher Education (2005) lists more than twenty states with reported increases of over 100 percent in their K–12 Latino population in the past ten years. The highest percentage increases are in regions not previously known for having large Latino communities, such as North Carolina (397 percent), Arkansas (309 percent), Georgia (301 percent), Tennessee (256 percent), and Nevada (248 percent). Obviously, legislative, community, and educational leaders within these states are concerned about the population shift and the impact it is having on their educational systems.

Ignoring the underrepresentation of Latinos in the education system is not in the best interest of the immediate communities, nor for the nation. In 1996, the President's Advisory Commission on Educational Excellence for Hispanic Americans noted that if Latinos attended college at the same rate as Whites, their earnings would grow by $118 billion and the nation's tax coffers would increase by $4 billion. The report recommended that efforts be made to close the gap between high school graduation and college-enrollment rates of Latinos to match those of White and Asian students. Unfortunately, as the numbers of White students enrolled in public colleges and universities has declined, so has the level of public financial support for higher education. The percentage of funds appropriated for higher education has declined in most states, and increases in tuition and fees have replaced the shortfall. The cost of attending a public college or university has outpaced most families' ability to pay, forcing students and their families to borrow heavily. The increasing level of debt facing students has discouraged many from selecting the institution of their choice and in some cases even the desire to seek college degrees at all.

As Latino faculty attempt to move up the academic pipeline, they face challenges and problems that non-Latino colleagues do not confront. Their academic credentials are questioned, the quality of their research and publications are challenged, and their academic contributions are often devalued because the work is not cited or published in traditional journals. Because many mainstream faculty lack the knowledge and experience of working with Latino publishers, journals, and associations, they fail to give equal treatment on decisions affecting their Latino colleagues' academic futures. Faculty and departments who are usually careful not to step beyond their areas of expertise often pass judgment on Latinos and their work without any reservations. Biases and misperceptions often result in Latino faculty being hired primarily in the fields of education, humanities, social sciences, and more specifically, in ethnic studies, Spanish, literature, and bilingual education programs.

A major problem facing higher education is the number of tenured faculty who are over the age of fifty-five who will be retiring in the near future. This trend also affects Latino faculty since many entered higher education in the 1970s under affirmative action and, given their scarcity in tenure-track positions and the time required to earn tenure, it is likely that the number of tenured Latino faculty will decline even more in the coming years.

With Latino students quickly becoming the majority group in key populous states and the projected increase in number of Latino faculty retiring, one would expect that developing Latino faculty would be a top priority.

The two most populous states, Texas and California, demonstrate the discrepancies that exist in faculty and administrative representation. These are the states with the largest Latino populations and which currently lead the nation in the representation of Latinos in higher education.

The Texas Perspective

Texas has the second largest and fastest growing Latino population in the nation, next to California (U.S. Census Bureau, 2005). Murdock (2004), a highly recognized demographer of Texas population, predicted decades ago that the population in Texas would double between 2000 and 2030, growing from 20.8 million to over 40.5 million. During this period Latinos are expected to increase from 32 percent to 54 percent (see Figure 4.1). The population of Whites is expected to increase; however, their percentage of the total population will decrease from 53 percent to 30 percent. Similarly, the number of Blacks will increase, but their percentage of the total population will decrease from 12 percent to 9 percent. The state's K–12 population is expected to increase from 3.3 million to 5.4 million. Latinos will account for the majority of the increase, and will exceed 54 percent of the K–12 population (Murdock, 2005).

Four-Year Public Institutions

At the university level, Texas has a highly diverse multiethnic and multilingual postsecondary student population, which is served by thirty-four, four-year public institutions, and seventy-six community colleges. In the fall of 2000, Whites accounted for 56 percent of the students enrolled in Texas public colleges and universities, and current projections are that by 2030 their representation will drop to 32 percent. During the same period, Latinos are expected to increase from 25 percent to 52 percent, which will make them the largest ethnic group, while Blacks are predicted to drop from 12 percent to 9 percent. In fall 2003, of 472,818 students enrolled in public four-year institutions, 99,544 were Latinos. At the public two-year institutions, of 536,005 students enrolled, 162,994 (30.4 percent) were Latinos. Among the degree recipients 12,212 (19.6 percent) of the 62,385 baccalaureate degrees awarded were earned by Latinos; 2,482 (12.6 percent) of the 20,199 master's degrees were Latinos, and 114 (5.7 percent) of the 1,992 doctoral degrees (Texas Higher Education Coordinating Board, 2004b).

As is true in most other states, Latinos are not as well represented in the tenured faculty as they are in the student bodies (see Figure 4.2). In the fall of 2003, 5.5 percent of tenured faculty at four-year public institutions were Latino, and 82 percent were

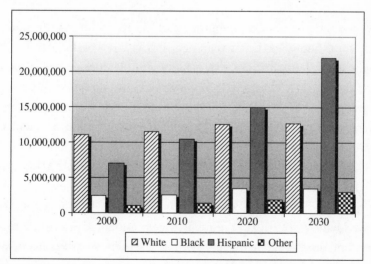

Figure 4.1. Texas Population Projection, 2000–2030
Source: Murdock (2003).
Note: Other category includes Asians.

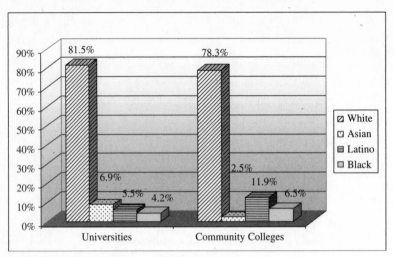

Figure 4.2. Texas Tenured Faculty

Source: Texas Higher Education Coordinating Board (2004a).

Notes: Total number of tenured university faculty = 8,983.

Total number of tenured community college faculty = 10,848.

White. The level of representation of White faculty is not much different than it was thirty years ago, and a review of the data shows that at most institutions the percentages of representation have not significantly changed. In reviewing the total representation of tenured faculty at public four-year institutions, we find that five campuses accounted for over half of the tenured Latino faculty. Twenty-one of the campuses reported ten or fewer tenured Latino faculty (Texas Higher Education Coordinating Board, 2004a).

At the university level, 11.8 percent of executive-level administrators during fall 2003 were Latino. Included in this group are individuals with titles of president, vice president, dean, and director, and mid-level managers with titles such as associate dean and assistant dean in academic departments. As with the tenured faculty positions, most Latino administrators are at a small number of campuses with over half of them employed at three campuses (Texas Higher Education Coordinating Board, 2004a).

Community Colleges

Though they serve a greater number of Latino students at community colleges, the Latino faculty there has not fared much better than at four-year institutions. In 2003 there were seventy-eight community colleges with 10,849 full-time faculty, of which 11.9 percent full-time Latino faculty and 78.2 percent full-time White faculty. As with the four-year institutions, a small number of campuses account for most of the Latino representation. Six community colleges accounted for over half of the Latino full-time faculty, with thirty-nine schools reporting ten or fewer Latino faculty members. The community colleges serve 536,005 students of whom 162,994 (30.4 percent) are Latino. They awarded 40,643 degrees and certificates of which 10,243 (25.2 percent) went to Latino students. The lack of adequate Latino faculty representation means that students do not have a chance to interact with Latino faculty or to hear their perspectives in their chosen academic fields (Texas Higher Education Coordinating Board, 2004a).

The level of representation of top Latino administrators at community colleges is similar to that of tenured faculty. Their numbers are small; they are concentrated in the student support service areas and are employed primarily at a handful of campuses. They are conspicuously underrepresented in most key academic positions. Of 1,592 administrators employed, 10.7 percent are Latino, and three campuses accounted for over half of the total number reported for the state. Although there has been a slight increase in the total number of Latinos selected as presidents of community colleges, the progress has been extremely slow and as the numbers demonstrate, it is inadequate (Texas Higher Education Coordinating Board, 2004a).

The California Perspective

If California were a nation, it would rank fifth in the world in its economy, agricultural products, technology, and numerous other areas (Assembly Office, 1986). For years, economic and social forecasters have used California as the bellwether state for monitoring trends for the rest of the nation. California has the nation's largest and fastest growing Latino population. From 1946 to 1963, California faced a population explosion, as the birth rates shot up during the "baby boomer" era. At that time, California responded to the educational needs of the baby boomers with what can best be described as visionary. In 1960, the legislature enacted the California Master Plan for Higher Education, which established a three-tier system that guaranteed high school graduates a tuition-free college education. The University of California (UC) with nine campuses served students who graduated in the top twelve percent of their high school classes. The California State Universities (CSU), with twenty-three campuses, served students who graduated in the top one-third, and the California Community Colleges (CCC), with over one hundred and eight campuses, served all high school graduates or the equivalent.

Today, educational demands have again reached unprecedented proportions similar to those that existed in the 1960s, the only differences being that Latinos are now the fastest growing population and the support to build new educational structures is not there. Data from the California Research Bureau State Library indicate that in 2002 the state of California had a population of 35.3 million of which four million were ages eighteen to twenty-five. Latinos accounted for 34 percent of the total population, and 43.5 percent of the eighteen- to twenty-five-year-olds. As mentioned earlier, California has the fastest growing population in the nation, and the projections are that by 2040 its population will exceed 56 million. By then, Latinos will account for over 50 percent of the population.

In 2002, the University of California system with its ten campuses (a new campus was added) employed 6,824 tenured faculty, of which Latinos accounted for 328 (4.8 percent) and

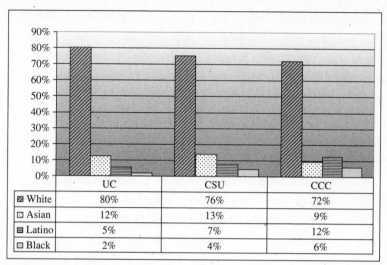

	UC	CSU	CCC
White	80%	76%	72%
Asian	12%	13%	9%
Latino	5%	7%	12%
Black	2%	4%	6%

Figure 4.3. California Tenured Faculty

Source: California Research Bureau (2001).

Notes: Total number of UC tenured faculty = 6,824.

Total number of CSU tenured faculty = 10,600.

Total number of CC tenured faculty = 12,524.

Whites accounted for 5,426 (80 percent) (see Figure 4.3). The percentage of White tenured faculty within the system has changed little from the 85 percent reported thirty-five years earlier. While the percentage of Latino tenured faculty increased during this period, from 2.8 percent to 4.8 percent, the level of representation achieved is not much to cheer about. These ten campuses have a student enrollment of 201,297, of which Latinos account for 11.4 percent, in a state where the Latino population will be the majority group by 2050 (Public Policy Institute, 1999).

The University of California in its admission information materials includes the following statement: "Mindful of its mission as a public institution, the University of California has had a historic commitment to providing a place within the University for all eligible applicants who are residents of California, and to achieving, on each campus, a student body that both meets the University's high academic standards and encompasses the cultural, racial, geographic, economic and social diversity of California itself." The wording makes clear that a top priority of the UC System is to enroll at each campus a student body of highly academically prepared students who reflect the diversity and cultural richness of the state. However, the commitment is for the system and not for individual campuses, which has resulted in a clustering of highly qualified minority students at certain UC campuses, while minority students remain seriously underrepresented at others.

The California State University (CSU) system's twenty-three campuses enrolled for Fall 2002 over 409,000 students, of which 82,006 were 20 percent Latino. The total number of tenured faculty for that semester was 10,600, of which Whites accounted for 8,004 (76 percent) and Latinos accounted for 706 (6.6 percent). The majority of tenured Latino faculty were at the assistant and associate levels, and only one campus had more than 10 percent Latino tenured faculty. The CSU system, whose main responsibility is teaching, has not done well in hiring and promoting Latino faculty. This is especially a problem for the nine campuses that are located in communities where over 40 percent of the population is Latino (Lopez & Rochin, 2001).

The California Community College (CCC) system is the largest two-year higher education system in the nation, providing courses to over 1.7 million students of which 30.4 percent are Latinos. The number of tenured faculty among the CCC campuses is 12,524, of which Latinos accounted for 1,502 (12 percent) of tenured faculty, and Whites accounted for 9,186 (73.3 percent). Since 1994, the combined percentage of Latinos, Asians, Blacks, and Native Americans has increased by only 4.3 percent. In reviewing the representation of administrators at CCC, the data show that between 1994 and 2002, the number of Whites increased the most (1,057 to 1,303), followed by Latinos (163 to 273) (Lopez, 2002).

Still Underrepresented After All These Years

While California and Texas are among the nation's leaders in serving Latinos in higher education, they still have a long way to go before they achieve what can be considered equitable representation. Most public leaders are aware of the growth and shift in their communities and recognize that Latinos need to obtain an education that is equal to the education received by the population they are replacing.

Unfortunately, higher education leaders appear complacent with the changing demographic situation and the role they must play. Most will acknowledge that the numbers for Latino faculty and administrators are lagging far behind population growth and student enrollment and admit that they do not foresee this changing in the immediate future. Most are knowledgeable of the data and the need for change, and use the information in spirited presentations at legislative hearings and community meetings when seeking funds. And over the years, funds have been approved to assist with the transition, and yet the gaps remain. It is clear that if change is going to occur, state legislators are going to have to take action as California did in the early 1960s and develop and fund comprehensive master plans that address the inadequacies that exist. This is not an easy task; historically, institutions of higher education have resisted any kind of change. The changes have to be more comprehensive than simply hiring a few more Latinos or upgrading the titles of those already in positions; it must include changes from the top to bottom of academia. Dr. Arturo Madrid, when he was president of the Tomas Rivera Center before it became the Policy Institute at USC, a think-tank on Latino policy issues, reminded us that: "We live in an age of continuous and intense change, a world in which what held true yesterday doesn't today and certainly won't tomorrow. What change does, moreover, is to bring about even more change. The only constant we have at this point in our national development is change. And change is threatening. It creates apprehension. It makes us nervous. The older we get the more likely we are to be anxious about change, the greater our desire to maintain the status quo" (Madrid, 1997).

The best way to handle the change generated by population growth is to be inclusive, which will allow the change to be gradual and molded by the contributions of diverse minds. This will develop a positive environment that will be accepting of a more pluralistic population. For forty years, institutions have been provided ample opportunities to make major changes by initiating strong affirmative action efforts. The Civil Rights Act of 1964, two executive orders, numerous federal court rulings, countless legislative mandates, federal- and state-funded programs, and pressure from community and political leaders provided justification for change. While most institutions applauded the federal court rulings and legislative efforts, most did not initiate any significant changes. However, when a regional court ruled in the *Hopwood vs. University of Texas* against certain affirmative action practices, most institutions moved expeditiously to comply with the ruling, abandoning affirmative action efforts. The Texas Attorney General, for example, issued instructions that went beyond the orders of the court.

Current models of educational success are based on past experiences which may not serve us well in the future, unless we allow for the tremendous changes and needs that a more diverse student body will bring. To some degree this issue was brought to national attention by the National Commission on Excellence in Education in their *Nation at Risk* report (1983). A key statement acknowledged the differences that were surfacing and the need for action:

> We do not believe that a public commitment to excellence and education reform must be made at the expense of a strong public commitment to equitable treatment of our diverse population. The twin goals of equity and high-quality schooling have profound and practical

meaning for our economy and society, and we cannot permit one to yield to the other either in principle or in practice. To do so would deny young people their chance to learn to live according to their aspirations and abilities. It also would lead to a generalized accommodation to mediocrity in our society on the one hand or the creation of an undemocratic elitism on the other." [p. 1]

The report also includes the well-known statement: "If an unfriendly foreign power had attempted to impose on America the mediocre educational conditions that exist today, we might well have viewed it as an act of war" (p. 5).

The educational conditions the commission found so alarming in the 1980s and viewed as a threat to the nation have not changed for Latinos. The statement recognized that those in higher education believe that quality and diversity could not co-exist. The report tried to reassure the public that diversity was important in higher education and in the best interest of all students and institutions. We find that the perception still exists in academia that increased diversity is achieved at the expense of quality and a threat to academic standards. Few mainstream academics acknowledge the legitimate academic contributions of Latinos by including them in their numerous presentations given at annual scholarly meetings throughout the country even though they voice a commitment to diversity.

Education Report Cards

I prepared a Texas Hispanic Report Card from 2003 to 2005 with the intent of focusing attention on the underrepresentation of Latinos at Texas public colleges and universities. The annual Texas Hispanic Report Card highlighted the lack of progress by institutions of higher education with regard to Latinos. The report card acknowledged the accomplishments of certain institutions and identified areas that required attention. It encouraged readers to not focus solely on the letter grades assigned to institutions, but to examine the statistical data, which provided a much more accurate perspective of Latino representation in higher education institutions. In most cases, the grades assigned were "kinder" than results reported because the majority of the campuses performed so poorly that over three-fourths of the campuses would have received failing grades. The report card brings immediate attention to the problems by showing the gains or lack of gains made by institutions.

The information used in preparing the Texas Hispanic Report Card was obtained from the Texas Higher Education Coordinating Board (www.thecb.state.tx.us) and reflects data submitted by the campuses. These data are gathered and reported in a prescribed format by the institutions and are available for each of the past ten years. Latinos from surrounding states have indicated great interest in developing similar report cards for their campuses. There are ongoing discussions among Latino leaders regarding the merits of establishing a southwestern regional report card that would allow the comparison among colleges and universities in the southwestern states.

As the Latino population moves from the role of minority to majority in schools and communities, it is important that public educational institutions remain committed to their initial design, which is to serve the public. State-funded colleges and universities, as public institutions, are supported by the public, for the good of the public, by educating students who return to their communities to provide needed services and develop opportunities for others. Today, the primary interest of many campuses is to become top-rated research institutions, and as a result they are becoming more selective in the students they recruit and admit. Most tier-one institutions enroll only top students, who are provided numerous opportunities to excel and achieve recognition that enhances the reputation of the institutions. This is done at the public expense by institutions that were initially designed to serve the general public. Most institutions and students no longer seem committed to honoring the concept of returning to serve the public, let alone the community that provided the opportunity for their education. Meanwhile, many of the communities faced with growing populations and increasing educational, employment, social, and medical needs do not benefit from the individuals educated in public institutions. Even if individuals wished to serve disadvantaged communities, they do not come from similar backgrounds or did not attend institutions with diverse student bodies and relevant curriculum, so they find the problems and environments so foreign that they give up quickly. Colleges and universities need to prepare their students so they can address the problems, issues, and challenges they will face when they enter the private or public sectors. Institutions of higher education need to hire faculty with whom students can identify and to offer an academic curriculum that relates to Latinos, the new majority.

With the optimism that a new century brings, we can dream of the important contributions Latinos will make to the future of the nation. In the coming years, the role of Latinos in many communities as leaders or followers will become increasingly important, and their successes or failures will depend on the education they receive now. While communities, cities, states, and the nation will survive with or without Latino involvement, it is in everyone's best interest if Latinos contribute to society as doctors, lawyers, teachers, and business owners, rather than as merely cheap laborers. If given the opportunity to fully participate at all levels of the educational pipeline, Latinos will succeed and will pave the way for others to follow.

5

Recent Strategies to Increase Access and Retention

Silas H. Abrego

This country's large corporations outsource work for two fundamental reasons, cost and a better educated workforce found outside the United States. Bill Gates, in a speech to the National Governor's Association at the National Education Summit on February 2005, stated that a high school education is obsolete. As he put it: "When I compare our high schools to what I see when I'm traveling abroad, I am terrified for our work force of tomorrow…. In 2001 India graduated almost a million more students from college than the United Stated did. China graduates twice as many students with bachelor's degrees as the U.S., and they have six times as many graduates majoring in engineering. In the international competition to have the biggest and best supply of knowledge workers, America is falling behind" (Gates, 2005).

In California, the Public Policy Institute of California (PPIC) reported that "one of the greatest threats facing the California economy is a projected shortage of college educated workers" (Campaign for College Opportunity, 2005, p. 1). For America to remain competitive it must educate the fastest growing pool of college-age students, Latinos. The growing number of Latinos in this country is dramatic; Latinos accounted for 36 percent of the 100 million added to the population in the last four decades (Pew Hispanic Center, 2006). Currently there are approximately 1.5 million Hispanic students enrolled in colleges and universities throughout the United States (U.S. Census Bureau, 2002). The national population of Latino students in college is expected to increase to 2.5 million by the year 2015 (De Los Santos & De Los Santos, 2003). Regardless of the numbers, Latinos continue to have low college participation rates. Clearly, we need to direct attention to graduating Latinos from college.

The keys to improving access to college for more Latinos and retaining those who enroll through to graduation are: (1) an understanding of their educational background coupled with strong academic and financial services; (2) a learning environment that encourages active learning; (3) and role models and activities that promote self-confidence. Moreover, it is essential that the campus community be willing to accept students at the level of preparedness they enter college with and commit themselves to educating the student from that level. To be sure, early academic preparation does make a difference in succeeding at the college level. However, because of the social and economic conditions in secondary schools that Latino students come from, many enter college underprepared.

Still, if the student does not enter with a 4.0 grade-point average and an SAT score of 1600, the faculty assume the quality of students is degenerating. These are the faculty who are wedded to the "sink or swim" pedagogy or the "I lecture you listen" methodology, both of which are ineffective and no longer viable. This reminds me of the humorous story of faculty members blaming the high school teachers for underprepared students. Of course, the high school teachers have to blame the elementary school teachers for not educating the students. Then, the elementary school teachers blame the parents for not getting their child school-ready. And then, from somewhere in the kitchen, you hear the mother-in-law saying, "Don't blame me, I was against the marriage in the first place!" My thinking and that of other Latino educators is that if the university accepts these students, then it is our responsibility to ensure a quality education for them and to provide the support to ensure their retention and graduation.

First-Generation Access Strategies

The rising enrollment of Latino youth in higher education is not only the result of more students in the secondary schools. One just needs to refer to the recent Harvard Civil Rights Project study of the Los Angeles Unified School District documenting a 37 percent drop-out rate to know that far too few are proceeding through the educational pipeline (Harvard Civil Rights Project, 2005). Other reports, such as *Leaks in the Chicana and Chicano Educational Pipeline* (Yosso & Solorzano, 2006), indicate that out of every one hundred elementary school Latino students, only forty-six eventually graduate with a high school diploma. And of the forty-six that do graduate, only nine enroll in a four year college. It has taken years of effort to achieve the number of Latino students that are now enrolled in higher education, and there is much more work still to be done.

Recruitment of Latino students started in earnest almost thirty years ago when a handful of Chicanos at southwestern higher education institutions organized themselves in order to open the campus up to others like themselves. Student organizations like Movimiento Estudiantil Chicano de Aztlán (MEChA) in California, the Mexican American Youth Organization (MAYO) in Texas, and the Mexican American Youth Association (MAYA) in Arizona designed recruitment programs, and got their universities to support and implement their outreach strategies. The program components these students developed are still being used today in many outreach programs. The primary task the students had at the time was to convince the higher education administration to be more inclusive, to promote higher education in the Latino communities as being attainable, to involve parents in discussing the right to a higher education, and to disseminate financial aid information.

Most important was the recognition that any discussion on the value of higher education needed to include the parents. Parents play an important role in influencing students' decision to attend college, particularly if they are low-income Latino students. Many working-class parents lack the necessary knowledge to guide their children to establish long-term educational goals. A major consideration for the parents is how to finance their children's higher education through scholarships, loans, and grants. Latino parents, regardless of income levels or educational attainment, want their children to succeed and have better opportunities than they had. It is not knowing how to help that is an obstacle for them. For this reason, effective outreach programs incorporate strong parental components.

One of the first organized programs was the Talent Search Program. This program was federally funded during President Johnson's Great Society years and is one of the TRIO programs. Talent Search was designed to spread the word in low-income communities about higher education opportunities. The program had an incredible impact because it came about during a time when most minority students were being tracked into vocational education courses in high school, and little or no information on higher education was reaching them. Talent Search reached almost all segments of the so-called "minority" communities and promoted the value of a higher education, informed students of the right to pursue higher education, and disseminated information on financial aid. Recruiters went to churches, parks, and shopping centers to reach these communities in general and parents in particular. Talent Search programs continue to exist and although they have evolved technologically, the fundamental emphasis on promoting the value of higher education, parent education, financial aid opportunities, and using Spanish for monolingual Spanish-speaking communities are still the building blocks of this successful outreach program.

The mission of Talent Search is to increase the number of students from disadvantaged backgrounds who complete their secondary education and continue on to postsecondary education. To accomplish this, Talent Search programs provide academic and support services. Academic services include academic counseling, skills development, tutoring, and academic monitoring. Support services include career workshops, personal counseling, lectures, educational trips to college campuses, and college application and financial aid assistance. These outreach services are provided to parents and families of students in the target areas.

The Upward Bound program is also part of TRIO. Upward Bound focuses on serving students at school and emphasizes academic preparation. The program identifies and recruits a group of students from targeted high schools and develops an Individual Education Plan for each student to track and evaluate his or her progress. Services include academic advising, after-school individual and group tutoring, educational field trips, summer residential programs on college campuses, personal counseling, financial aid and college admissions workshops, college application assistance, SAT test preparation workshops, career exploration workshops, and a strong parent component including parent workshops and an Upward Bound Family Day. The program provides Saturday Enrichment Sessions and after-school sessions to reinforce the school-based curriculum and to prepare students for success in secondary school and beyond. As mentioned earlier, the leakage in the pipeline from ninth grade through twelfth grade is significant; this program directs students through high school graduation up to eligibility for college in a seamless manner. Upward Bound continues to make its contribution in preparing young people to pursue higher education.

Second-Generation Access Strategies

As effective as TRIO has been, the need to reach more students is necessary. Federal funding will not meet the needs of the growing number of students requiring the services. As a result, newly formed partnerships between local schools and colleges are becoming more common. Partnerships also tend to sustain change regardless of the continuance of special funding. The newly funded GEAR UP program is an illustration of the types of partnerships being formed to increase the number of first-generation, low-income students in higher education. GEAR UP has a mission similar to Talent Search and Upward Bound, but the program methodology is more encompassing. GEAR UP targets a seventh-grade cohort and serves the same student cohort through high school graduation. It also combines a parent education component, educational field trips, tutoring, and adds a teacher in-service component to enhance teachers' skills in core curriculum to better prepare students for higher education. An important program element of GEAR UP is the requirement of matching funds from the institutions, and required participation from local government and businesses, and community-based organizations. The National Council for Community and Education Partnerships has taken the leadership role in guiding the development and operation of partnerships in the country and advocating for continued program funding.

One of the most successful privately funded partnership programs is the ENLACE program. ENLACE is the acronym for Engaging Latino Communities for Education and the word *enlace* in Spanish means "to weave together." This is a W.K. Kellogg Foundation initiative to increase the educational attainment of Latino students. Kellogg awarded $28 million to various institutions across the country to develop and implement local strategies that would involve various community agencies in improving education for Latinos. The Santa Ana, California, ENLACE program provides a good model of how whole communities can become involved in improving education for Latino students.

The Santa Ana ENLACE Partnership was established as a collaboration between the Santa Ana Unified School District, Santa Ana College, California State University-Fullerton, the University of California-Irvine, and community-based organizations to strengthen the educational pipeline from high school through to graduate school and increase opportunities for Latinos to enter and complete college. According to the original proposal, the "Santa Ana ENLACE Blueprint for Change focuses [its] efforts in a partnership that coordinates and sustains system-wide and inter-segmental policies and practices to improve student performance at key transition points along the educational pipeline" (Santa Ana ENLACE, 2005). These goals are being accomplished through a clear set of objectives to increase academic achievement, college preparation and eligibility, college-going and enrollment rates, transfer rates, retention and graduation rates, as well as the number of Latino students who continue on to graduate education.

Outreach programs conceived through collaborations or partnerships with other agencies have a better chance of being mainstreamed and having their goals reflected in institutional mission statements. To be sure, there are numerous projects that are effective in preparing students to succeed in college. In fact, at every higher education professional organization conference there are workshops, panels, and speakers reporting on good practices that lead to improving the college's prospects of succeeding with low-income historically underrepresented students. However, most of these programs, because of their funding sources, operate independently and are often isolated by the institutions. As a result, they don't have the leverage to influence educational practices on their respective campuses. Collaborative efforts will have a greater ability to change institutional behaviors regarding academic preparation of students.

For this reason, Santa Ana ENLACE created a collection of targeted programs and services to be implemented by the higher education partners. In the past, individual programs being implemented separately by multiple institutions of higher education in the same community became fragmented, and the impact was dispersed. Collaboratives enable partners to bring together resources in a coordinated manner and draw on the strengths that each partner has to offer. Below are a few highlights of the Santa Ana ENLACE Partnership. The types of services provided should be integrated into any effective outreach effort in other communities:

Higher Education Centers. These centers were created at each of the Santa Ana high schools to be one-stop information and service centers for high school counselors, teachers, parents, and students. Higher Education Center Specialists provide information on financial aid, the college application process, as well as academic and test preparation. The higher education partners designate liaisons from their campuses to provide on-site support at the centers, including on-site admissions, college information and materials, and participation in college nights.

MESA. The Mathematics, Engineering, and Science Achievement program identifies and supports students interested in pursuing careers in science, engineering, or math by providing discipline-specific tutoring and mentoring opportunities. Special sections of math and science courses, a pathway for future math and science teachers, special discipline-specific conference experiences, and summer research opportunities are all part of this intensive program.

Puente. This program provides focused support and mentoring, including academic and cocurricular support services, to Latino K–12 and first-generation community college students to promote and ease their transition to the next level in the educational pipeline.

College Now. Santa Ana College offers college classes to students at the Santa Ana high schools that allow them to earn college credit while still attending high school. This enhances the students' transition to higher education by providing exposure to college courses.

Padres Promotores de la Educación. This program recruits parents from the community who serve as liaisons and outreach to other parents through nontraditional methods, such as home visits, working with existing neighborhood associations, and informal educational dialogues. Through these means, parents receive accurate and relevant information about higher education.

Latino Baccalaureate and Beyond, and Bridge to the Doctorate. Through these two programs, the three higher education partners, Santa Ana College, University of California-Irvine, and California State University-Fullerton, work to increase the number of Latino students who continue to graduate school. They also provide information about graduate school requirements, available opportunities, and barriers that they need to overcome.

Of course these are only a few highlights, and there are many more programs being implemented at the school district level and by the higher education partners to improve academic preparation and college preparatory course completion to accomplish the ambitious goals of Santa Ana ENLACE. The Santa Ana ENLACE Partnership ended its initial five-year cycle of funding in 2006 and began Phase III ENLACE, which has the goal of sustaining a statewide partnership that is charged with increasing the success of Latino students, and others, along the P–20 educational pathway. This will be accomplished by creating, developing, and sustaining bridges between the various segments of the P–20 system and sharing best practices learned through the various ENLACE partnerships.

One additional component to consider in any outreach program is a transitional focus. Transitional focus provides students with exposure to a higher education environment. Students have the opportunity to experience the college curriculum, teaching styles, and class workload. First-generation college students particularly need to be familiarized with higher education early on. The summer programs also allow the students opportunities to begin building a network of friends and adjusting socially. The Summer Bridge Program in California is an example of a successful summer transitional program.

Summer Bridge is designed for incoming, low-income students who are considered at-risk academically. At California State University-Fullerton, Summer Bridge is an intensive six-week residential program that combines course work with personal growth and academic survival skills instruction. Through this program, students develop a peer network, are exposed to the many resources on campus, and work toward completing remediation that may be required in a supportive environment. Students are then tracked into other support programs to ensure they receive services to ensure their persistence.

Through ENLACE funding, students transferring from Santa Ana College to the University of California-Irvine have the opportunity to participate in a similar transition program, the Summer Scholars Transfer Institute. Students are provided an intensive ten-day residential institute to complete core academic transfer courses. Instructional teams are developed for each course including faculty, counselors, and teaching assistants, and each class forms its own learning community.

Through all of these types of outreach and transitional programs, Latino students are becoming more informed regarding higher education, better prepared, and enrolling in postsecondary education at higher rates. The next step is effectively retaining those students as they begin to enter college campuses across the nation and ensuring they graduate.

Retention Programs

Regardless of the strong early preparation programs, Latino students still have a difficult time acclimating to a college environment. Many are first in their families to attend college and therefore unfamiliar with the social and academic demands of a college education.

If the campus has not evolved to meet the needs of students of diverse backgrounds, the student will feel isolated, unwanted, and eventually withdraw from the campus. Successful institutions make it clear in their mission statement that they embrace and appreciate diversity. They demonstrate their commitment to having a diverse faculty, staff, and strong ethnic studies programs and resource centers. Additionally, they maintain strong ties with the local community and make them feel the university is there to serve them. The successful campus develops and sustains partnerships with local community agencies and schools. Moreover, it initiates and supports numerous academic support services, particularly in the difficult majors like math and science, which enhances the student's chances for graduation. And, it does matter that the president, and other high-level administrators, including faculty leadership, continuously promote and reward individuals involved in graduating students of color. Regrettably, after forty years of assertive action, there are too few institutions which sustain these characteristics.

Retention starts with an effective new student orientation program that clearly addresses the challenges students will face. These programs should not assume that students are familiar with college life. Low-income students, and in particular first-generation college students, are concerned with financial aid, employment opportunities, academic support programs, meeting individuals from similar backgrounds, and explaining to their parents the time demands of a college education. It is important that during new student orientation students are introduced to juniors and seniors with similar backgrounds to share their stories of surviving on campus. It will relieve a lot of stress for students and at the same time allow them to start developing a support network.

A program targeted at first-year students is also a good retention tool. Through a University 100 class or a Freshman Experience Program, students are part of a supportive learning community during their first year of higher education. Students are provided with information to successfully navigate the college campus, are exposed on an ongoing basis to campus resources, and are provided skill development.

A support network comprised of staff, faculty, and peers is crucial to the student's ability to successfully navigate the campus. Students who can act as peer mentors can help guide freshmen to various offices and serve as part of their support network. Staff members can play an important role in their support network, particularly if they have contacts in the financial aid office, career center, learning center, and in the areas of student life. Faculty can be a major factor in a student's support network. Almost all of us who have successfully graduated from college can identify one faculty member who made a difference in our educational career, either by inspiring us, believing in our potential, or being a role model. It is important the student understand there is a formal network comprised of traditional offices and an informal network comprised of individuals on campus who can advocate on their behalf. Knowing the informal network can at times be more effective than knowing the traditional offices and services.

An effective retention program will have a vehicle in place to detect early whether a particular student is having difficulty. Early detection is essential to "saving" a student rather than trying to save someone who is facing the academic disqualified list. Identifying students' weaknesses early will allow the college to refer them for tutoring, to the learning center, or to a mentor. The Student Support Services (SSS) Program is one of the TRIO programs that encompasses all of the ingredients of a successful retention program and can serve as a model.

Student Support Services has a particular focus on the retention and graduation of low-income, first-generation, or disabled students. To ensure the success of these students, SSS provides a number of targeted services that promote the requisite skills and motivation. Services include (1) personal counseling, academic and career advisement, (2) learning skills, study skills, and personal development workshops, (3) study groups and tutorial services, (4) mentoring, and (5) financial aid advisement.

Personal counseling and academic advisement are targeted at helping students to achieve their personal and academic goals. During individual counseling and advisement sessions, students are given the opportunity to clearly map out their academic path, articulate their career goals, and discuss any ongoing challenges they may be having to facilitate early detection. Counselors develop an Individual Education Plan (IEP) for each student. They closely monitor students' academic progress, analyze student needs, assist in course selection, and help students interpret college rules and regulations. Counselors provide specialized attention to students who are enrolled in remedial courses to ensure they complete those courses and to those who are on or approaching academic probation or disqualification which disproportionately affects low-income students. Referrals to other campus offices and agencies are provided, as well as information about graduate education and required exams. This individualized attention is important for high-risk students who are often the first in their family to attend college and who may be lacking in academic preparation. It creates an ongoing mechanism to ensure students are retained.

In addition, many students need assistance to develop more effective learning and study skills, and workshops are an effective way to provide this training to groups of students. Faculty and staff throughout the university facilitate workshops targeted at helping students improve their study strategies, note taking, listening and writing skills, overcome anxieties (such as in mathematics and test taking), and teaching students research techniques. Workshops targeted at personal development are also important for students. Topics may include adjusting to college, goal setting and career planning, money management, stress management, and health awareness. Each of these areas of focus helps students to be more confident and successful in their coursework, usually resulting in improved grades and course completion.

Another way academic performance is improved is through study groups and tutoring. These components help students to better understand their course assignments and seek clarification when necessary. Students develop study plans that are specific to their particular course. Study groups also create a peer network that fosters learning and academic improvement. Students can compare notes, discuss assignments, improve study skills, and prepare for tests. An effective campus Learning Center can provide these services as well as targeting a multitude of coursework and providing tutoring in challenging upper division courses and opportunities for collaborative learning. Tutors have specific content knowledge and are sensitive to the needs of low-income, first-generation students.

A mentoring component is also an integral element of SSS. Mentors are particularly important for Latino students who are often the first in their families to attend college and do not have role models who can help them understand what to expect and how to effectively navigate a college campus. Mentoring programs should make an effort to recruit faculty and staff who are from similar backgrounds as the student population and who are sensitive to the cultural and social experiences that have shaped the students through their early education. Mentors teach students to be more comfortable approaching faculty and staff, which helps them be more confident in their classes and better engaged in their education.

Also it is particularly important for students to understand their financial aid options. Many low-income students are unfamiliar with the various ways they can find assistance to fund their education, and finances can become an insurmountable barrier. As a result, retention programs should demystify the financial aid process so students can clearly understand the different types of aid available to them and how to apply in order to receive maximum aid. Through the SSS program, students are made aware of what they need to do in order to remain eligible for financial aid. In addition, students are provided guidance in finding and applying for the many private and university scholarships that are available, and they are provided assistance in preparing effective financial aid and scholarship applications.

A final component of SSS that should be part of the college culture is encouraging students to aspire not only for a baccalaureate degree but for graduate and professional degrees. SSS works collaboratively with another federally funded TRIO program, the Ronald E. McNair Postbaccalaureate Achievement Program. The McNair Program provides low-income, first-generation students underrepresented in graduate school with the preparation necessary to pursue and succeed in graduate school. Students enrolled in the program are provided with the opportunity to conduct research with a faculty mentor in their field, to prepare a research paper of publishable quality and present their work at a conference, and are helped through the graduate school research and application process.

In addition, staff from the McNair Program make presentations to students in other retention programs throughout the campus regarding the benefits of and requirements necessary to enroll in graduate school. Students are educated regarding how to find a graduate school program that fits their academic and personal goals and interests. Faculty and staff throughout the campus are also available to present workshops, and a graduate school symposium is held on campus to ensure that all students are exposed to graduate school information.

Each of these services—from academic counseling to financial aid assistance—is crucial for improving campus retention rates. Students need to be supported in all areas of their personal, academic, and career development, and they need to be aware of the resources available on campus to help them achieve their educational goals. Elements in federally funded TRIO programs must become institutionwide, and a culture of targeted support for all students must be fostered at universities to improve retention rates of Latino students.

Summary

We use the TRIO programs to illustrate program components that have been effective over time in meeting the needs of low-income, first-generation college students. In fact, several of TRIO's program concepts have been adopted by a second-generation of programs as strategies that can serve all students. Campus learning centers, peer mentoring programs, faculty or staff mentoring programs, and learning skills development workshops all have their genesis in TRIO programs. However, like other categorical and specially funded programs, institutions have been slow to embrace and mainstream them to serve all students. The challenge these programs face is that once the funds run out, the services are gone and there is no sign they ever existed. However, not to sustain these programs and mainstream them to serve all students will be more costly for this country in the long run. If higher education ignores the Latino segment of the population, it will not be able to compete internationally and will have failed in developing our greatest resource, the new majority of Latino students.

6

Latino Professional Associations
Advocacy for Liberation

Leonard A. Valverde

Transforming higher education institutions so that they better serve Latino students, who in turn can help to meet the growing needs of Latino communities, is the main goal of Latino higher education and K–12 professionals. The formation of professional associations with a particular focus has been a strategy used by many other groups to advance their cause. Before the 1960s, most Latino advocacy groups were community based and targeted to social issues, such as the League of United Latin American Citizens (LULAC) started in 1929 and the G.I. Forum founded in 1948. With the advent of the Civil Rights movement, Latino educators began to come together at annual meetings of professional organizations. As a critical, albeit small, core of Latinos began to emerge, caucuses were organized within already established national associations, such as the American Association for Higher Education. As the number of Latino faculty, administrators, and staff began to increase in higher education, due mostly to the civil rights struggles, a few efforts were initiated to form stand-alone Latino professional associations, such as the Texas Association of Chicanos in Higher Education (TACHE) in 1974 and the Hispanic Association of Colleges and Universities (HACU) in 1986. Today we have a number of formal subgroups within traditional professional associations, for example the National Community College

Hispanic Council (NCCHC) of the American Association of Community Colleges (AACC); more community-based associations with an educational emphasis such as ASPIRA, the Mexican American Legal Defense and Educational Fund (MALDEF), and the National Council of La Raza; and other educational groups, such as the Association of Mexican American Educators (AMAE), the Arizona Association of Chicanos for Higher Education (AACHE), the Mexican American School Board Members Association, and the Association of Latino Superintendents and Administrators.

Each of the professional associations has made a contribution in improving the education of Latinos. This chapter is written to stimulate new thinking about the roles Latino professional associations can play and what they can do in the future. The contents should not be viewed as criticism of any existing association. The intent and spirit is to offer suggestions of what associations need to do to be even more successful in the future.

In this chapter, I will not enumerate or discuss the various tasks that professional organizations do to fulfill their missions, such as generating publications, holding annual conferences, giving awards, conducting training sessions, offering testimony before public bodies, formulating policy recommendations, and so on. The suggestions offered can and should be translated into concrete action. I firmly believe we have leaders in the field that can envision the ideas and put them into practice. So while this chapter should not be considered a road map, it certainly is directed at creating collective action that will strengthen Latino associations and propel our agenda for improvement.

The Value of Professional Organizations

Before proceeding to the suggestions, some observations are in order. First, Latino professional associations were created primarily out of need. For the most part, at the start of these associations, a small number of founders came together to initiate an association because of a common set of expectations and aspirations to improve conditions for Latino students and correct negative professional experiences. These common aspirations, which typically became the group's mission statement, and common negative experiences attracted membership. Second, professional associations form to offer knowledge, protection, and motivation to their members and leaders. Within associations, members can learn from each other, speak freely and openly, challenge the ineffective status quo of institutions, and share success stories, all of which attracts members. Third, professional associations can take action to leverage change at more than one institution and influence public policy makers to act by mobilizing association members. Last, professional associations liberate their members by allowing them to voice their opinions and apply their intellectual talent, without fear of institutional backlash.

Latino Professional Associations

Latino professional associations were started because institutions of higher education and existing professional associations were not attending to Latino issues in a satisfactory way. These educational institutions and associations continue to see Latinos as only a small and unimportant part of a larger problem. Because we have made some progress, although still insufficient, and we know what can and should be done, Latino professional associations must consider working differently than in the past. Even though a number of our Latino/a brothers and sisters are presidents or chancellors of colleges and universities, governance and bureaucracy have continued to restrict them from doing what needs to be done. Hence, our Latino higher education leaders can use Latino professional associations to articulate a transformation agenda and challenge the status quo.

Building More Effective Associations

Following are twelve proposals for making Latino professional associations more effective. Not all will apply to every association, and some associations are doing some of the suggestions already. Depending upon an association's particular status, each recommendation has a different value, hence they are not offered in order of importance. Metaphorically, they are presented in the style of "moving away from" and "closer to" something.

From Concern About Numbers to Concern About Ideas

We have come to believe that numbers mean power. We have also learned that this axiom works at times, but not as often for Latinos as we would like and certainly not like it works for others, especially Whites. Despite this knowledge, we overly rely on the numbers game. In our professional associations, this translates into adding more members. We like to be able to say that our membership is large and growing (and all that an increase in membership may represent). More members also means more revenue for the association through dues and registration fees at annual conferences. While membership is important and requires constant attention, we should not be distracted from directing our efforts toward generating ideas, voicing our mission, and calling for action. In fact by doing these things, the association stands a far greater chance of attracting new members and maintaining current membership. Also as professional associations continue year after year, they tend to stray from their main mission, not so much in concept but in what they attend to, such as planning activities, events, and committees. Both leadership and long-standing members are responsible for staying true to the mission and reminding newcomers of the priorities, issues, and concerns that must be attended to on an annual basis. We have too little human capital to waste on tangential items.

From Unilateral to Relational Power

As professionals, we have been socialized to the workings of professional associations through firsthand experience. Therefore like many others, we base our organizations on familiar models. Given that traditional associations have large memberships and are well respected, we may conclude that they are the models to copy. However, there are differences between traditional associations and Latino associations. Traditional professional associations are compatible with and complement institutions. Our Latino agenda, issues, and concerns challenge institutions to change. Therefore, in one fundamental respect, our purpose is different from that of the traditional professional associations. Traditional professional associations use unilateral power (Cortes, 1993) by practicing the power of persuasion and indirectly reminding institutions that their large membership is represented on their campuses. Clearly, while the concerns and issues voiced by our fledgling associations are on high moral ground, getting institutions to respond fully or sincerely has been slow and difficult. There is an unequal relationship between Latino professional associations and White institutions, thus the unilateral influence does not work (Warren, 2005). Therefore, we must consider using both unilateral power and relational power. By relational, we mean getting things done in cooperation with others. Specifically, we need to organize the social capital of our community to leverage both the political arena and economic sector to help us influence institutions and their power brokers.

From Describing Problems to Exposing Causes

With technology making it relatively easy to collect demographic information and other types of data, many professional organizations are producing reports that highlight the Latino plight in society and in higher education. The Western Interstate Commission for Higher Education in Colorado and the Center for Advancement of Racial and Ethnic Equality within the

American Council on Education, for example, have documented the demographic data and the lack of relative and substantial improvement when compared to our population growth. For Latino associations to remind people of our condition is of little value when others are doing such a good job of providing data. A few of the established professional national associations have formed committees to examine the demographics and issue recommendations. Too often, these committees have insufficient Latino representation or able to produce a report that list recommendations equal to the scope of the problems.

Hence, I propose that our Latino organizations apply themselves to do what others do not do enough of or do not do well. Latino associations should communicate to the public by way of presentations why the demographic data are so alarming; identify what we need to do at the institutional level, ensure better Latino representation in higher education, not just as students, but also as professional support staff, faculty, and administrators; and finally recommend solutions that are commensurate with the scope of the problems. Our members have not only the ideas but the working solutions. We know, through our collective experiences, not only how to generate greater access, but how to retain students and faculty as well. Our solutions will carry more value if we can get the established professional associations to endorse our hard-hitting ideas of what needs to get done.

From Posturing to Positioning

Sometimes we may try to project an image of major importance to an established professional organization we are attempting to influence in the hopes they will take our recommendations seriously. A Latino president or executive director may posture just for show when attending meetings with other administrators. Unfortunately, spending valuable time on posturing yields few results. It is too superficial and a token action, a photo moment. Therefore, Latino organizations should turn their efforts to position themselves as leaders by developing a track record of taking action on important issues and by joining with other influential stakeholders, like Congressional representatives who are already sympathetic to these issues. Posturing is superficial and positioning is substantive. The former yields few outcomes. The latter has the potential of producing something tangible and potentially lasting.

From Being Reactive to Being Proactive

Because our associations are understaffed or staffed by a few volunteers, we are placed in a mode of having to react to unforeseen developments or spontaneous "brush fires" at institutions. These may involve comments made by a significant person at a major gathering or a book that perpetuates the stereotypes that we have had to endure and overcome. Some of these statements are too difficult to let go unchallenged. So if we want to join in the counteraction, our associations need to establish a process that can be activated without much effort or delay, such as designating beforehand a person to draft a short but pointed response, or having a newspaper outlet ready to print a response.

For a group to be proactive, I recommend that the group's leadership hold a two-day retreat, where the year's goals are planned, calendar set, and annual logistics assigned. This is not a retreat to map out the traditional events, like the publication of newsletters or to decide on the theme of the annual conference. This retreat should promote deep discussion of important concerns and determine how the organization can be instrumental in changing institutions.

From Working Separately to Connecting and Cooperating

The sad fact is there are too many things to attend to, and too few of our Latino professional organizations are staffed sufficiently to get things done in a timely manner, let alone in a forceful fashion. Hence we either have to set priorities and stay true to those priorities or enlarge our capacity so we can attend to more matters. Given my experience, there are too many items to attend to and we believe we must address them all. Since it is highly unlikely that our professional associations are going to increase the operating budget overnight, the way to enhance our capacity is to connect with other associations who are working on the same agenda items. This way, we do the piece of the work we know best and let other associations do the piece they know best. In so doing, we can get more accomplished as well as grow in influence.

From Short- to Long-Term Efforts

Most of our associations are governed by elected persons who serve for a year. As a result, the association's calendar is limited to a year. Continuation of past efforts is often limited to operations, such as the annual conference, membership drive, newsletters, and so on. Annual conference themes are rarely carried forward, since committees are appointed usually for one year and are typically ad hoc and do not continue under a newly elected head. This type of short-term planning and annual operation may allow the functioning of the association, but it only partially taps the capability of the association. We must remember that the lack of sufficient access, retention, and successful graduation of Latino students is an ongoing struggle. Therefore, we must develop a new mindset with a longer calendar and underlined with persistence. We should establish standing committees that produce reports and are responsible for updating the reports annually, reflecting progress or lack thereof by institutions. We must identify objectives, not goals, that have a three- to four-year working time line. We must engage with institutions to provide technical assistance, such as program design, policy revisions, and so on over a three- to four-year period of time.

From Joining the Parade to Leading the Parade

Posturing and working alone are not effective ways of utilizing our limited talent pool. Instead, we must position ourselves and connect with others. Not only should we connect with others of like mind and contribute our expertise, but we should marshal our talented members to interact with other prominent and well-established groups. Through their individual achievements and successes many of our members are deans, vice presidents, or presidents of institutions. These association members should be asked to serve as chairs of major taskforces. Our associations can also identify a specific agenda item that has multiple facets and then develop a strategy to elicit other professional associations to join our taskforce.

From Routine Ceremonies to Public Recognition

Most associations give out awards and sponsor ceremonies to recognize persons for their achievements. While these ceremonial events are valuable, our Latino associations need to capitalize on these social events. These routine ceremonies should symbolize what the association holds as highly desirable. Ceremonies should be a way to drive nonmembers and institutions toward modeling what we want campuses and institutional staff, faculty, and administrators to do. Add meaning and prestige to the award by communicating what the award stands for and why the recipient rightfully deserves it. Be certain to publicize these events and get wide coverage. A good example of this approach was the creation of the Tomas Rivera Lecture at the annual American Association of Higher Education (AAHE) conference. This event was well publicized in the program, well attended, and had high-profile speakers. To remember Tomas Rivera and what he stood for, the focus of the speaker's comments had to address diversity in higher education. The content of the presentation was reported in the association's annual proceedings. Regrettably, this is no more with the demise of AAHE in 2005.

From Superficial Concerns to Substantive Concerns

Once any organization or association becomes established, routine often takes precedence. As people assume roles either through annual elections or long-term appointments, following a set pattern without thinking becomes the norm. While this approach assures the day-to-day things get done, loss of focus on meaningful items also occurs. Thus Latino associations need to go beyond routine and center themselves on substance, what matters most. This can be done by conducting an annual retreat of the elected officers, board members, and staff for at least one full day and preferably two. Another way is to hold an open forum at the annual conference, and a third way is to survey members periodically via the association's Web page. This data collection and brainstorming should be incorporated in long-term planning, follow-up, and assessment of progress.

From Imbalance to Balance

The majority if not all of the Latino professional associations were started to advocate for better treatment of their constituents and for the improvement of education across the country. In their early days, Latino associations held to strong stances. At times, we had to confront our "adversaries" and push our official representatives or friends to be more visible or vocal. With the passage of time, association membership and elected leadership may become more moderate and conciliatory. Fortunately, none of our associations has strayed from its original intent. Associations go through phases, shifting from aggressive to passive, but we do not have the luxury of lapsing into moderation. At best we must be able to maintain a duality or balance. We must be prepared to confront the power holders, especially when these elites continue to refuse to respond to reason.

From a Closed to an Open System

Too often association leaders form cliques. It matters little how long one has been a member or how well one has served. An invitation to the inner circle often depends on who you know or if you hold an executive position at a college or university. Such a member may suddenly get instant credibility and be elected into a position of leadership within the association. Or a member who has paid his or her dues over time but was rarely involved in the association may be elected because the former leadership knows him or her. Under such circumstances, the association became a "closed" operation. Remember most if not all of the Latino professional organizations were formed because we, as individual members, belonged to national associations who ignored or devalued our educational condition or plight. In essence, they were closed to us! We need to stay true to being open, to fully tapping our members, to harness our interested and talented *colegas* (colleagues), to solicit suggestions, to encourage ideas, involve our new *gente* (people) in the profession, to examine criticism, and so on. Only by staying open will our Latino associations be able to sustain and replenish themselves.

How to Increase Time, Effort, and Quality

While many of the Latino higher education associations would like to do more, they are restricted by lack of staff, specifically paid staff. Professionals often volunteer a small portion of their institutional time or after-work hours to deal with association issues. Even for those associations who do have paid staff members, there are too few personnel and too many tasks to attend to. So without the infusion of funds, what can be done?

1. As the baby boomer population ages, a growing number of Latinos in higher education are starting their retirement. Many of these recent retirees have been in executive positions and have large networks. They should be invited to contribute their knowledge to help move the organization's agenda forward. It is important to match the task to the person's talent. We don't want to underutilize or insult them. For example, a retired president or vice president of an institution could be asked to serve as the executive director on a quarter- or half-time basis.

2. Those elected to the organization's head positions should ask for some release time from their institutions, as is typically done for professors at major four-year institutions. For example, a faculty member who becomes an editor of a journal typically gets released from teaching a course and at some institutions is provided office space, computer, telephone access, postage, and so on.

3. As we all know, there are many more Latinos and especially Latinas who are studying toward master and doctoral degrees. Our professional organizations should seek these students out (especially those within driving distance to the association headquarters) and explore ways of incorporating them into the association. These graduate students can do an internship for course credit; get help in writing term papers in return for their services; or the institution can pay them as work study students.

4. By joining with another group on a common agenda item, we can share resources or at the very least cut back the amount of time needed by acting separately.

Conclusion

Latino professional associations are first and foremost advocacy agents. Their main purpose is to advance the interest of *nuestra gente*, to guard against intrusions on our rights by well-established institutions of higher education, and to protect us from discrimination by governing bodies and elected representatives. Since our status has remained for the most part flat (as documented by this book), we, through our own organizations, need to push the envelope to the full extent. I state the obvious because some of us may lose sight of our people's lack of progress. As professionals in academia we have been successful individually (completing advanced degrees and moving up the higher education ladder as staff, faculty, or administration), and we may begin to rationalize our people's condition and in so doing, temper our efforts, particularly with institutions.

When we gather together in our associations, we hear other voices, such as those of students and community members, who remind us that our agenda of greater access and success in the academy inches slowly ahead. In listening to those voices, we stay true to our original purpose. Hence it is vital that our professional associations express our dissatisfaction and, more important, promote viable solutions. And yes, even if this translates into identifying those institutions and leaders who continue to resist in order to shame them, we should do so.

Just as we are calling for colleges and universities to remake themselves to better serve our future generation of students and communities, so too must we rethink how we organize ourselves to be more effective. History tells us that persons of color will have to fight to gain their full and equal rights. Let our Latino professional associations lead the struggle for liberation. As the old rhythm and blues song goes, "give me the people and free my soul."

7

Establishing Institutions of Higher Education That Serve Latinos

Monte E. Perez

Higher education institutions are not serving the needs of Latinos in the United States. Latinos remain underrepresented at a time when they are the largest minority in the United States and the fastest growing segment of the population. The federal government over time has responded by providing student financial assistance, sponsoring federally funded Title V, Hispanic-Serving Institutions (HSI) programs for colleges and universities with 25 percent or more Hispanic students, and by supporting various academic and student support programs like TRIO to help Latinos and traditionally underrepresented groups succeed.

Although these efforts have met with some success, they continue to be ineffective in meeting the overall need for access, retention, and graduation of Latinos in higher education. Latinos continue to confront barriers in access. Not only do Latinos confront financial barriers, they also have difficulty integrating socially on college campuses and are severely underprepared academically. Latinos are not persisting in college and completing their academic goals at a sufficient rate. Many institutions admit Latinos but do not do an effective job in keeping them and ensuring that they succeed. Finally, Latinos are not graduating in sufficient numbers. Campuses enroll Latinos but are not held accountable for the graduation and completion of degrees.

This is happening at a time when the Latino population is reaching an all-time high in the United States. In the last five years, one out of every two new Americans was Latino, and in the southeastern part of the United States unprecedented growth of the Latino population has occurred. The report "The New Latino South" (Kochhar, Suro, & Tafoya, 2005) focuses on six southern states: Alabama, Arkansas, Georgia, North Carolina, South Carolina, and Tennessee. Each state experienced tremendous growth from 1990 to 2000, exceeding 1000 percent in some counties. The report predicts that by 2007 the population of Latino children, which grew more than 320 percent, will make up 10 percent of the students in the southeastern public schools, and this demographic wave will hit colleges and universities in the region soon thereafter. States with high Latino population, such as California, Arizona, New Mexico, Texas, Illinois, Florida, and New York, face serious budgetary and policy challenges to effectively serve Latinos. These challenges are not being met with long-term planning and policy development. In fact, states are trying to meet the needs of Latinos incrementally and ineffectively by instituting special-funded programs and services on a piecemeal basis. It is time for states to develop comprehensive policies.

This chapter argues for some new definitions to evaluate Latino success in higher education. It recommends some bold initiatives to help meet the higher education needs of Latinos. The chapter examines the role of the states in promoting access, retention, and graduation of Latinos. California, the nation's largest system serving Latinos, serves as a prime example of how state higher education institutions are not meeting the needs of Latinos.

Key Issues Preventing Latinos from Succeeding in Higher Education

Lack of Participation

A recent report by the California Public Policy Institute stated that "in the next fifteen years, the job market is expected to change so dramatically in California that the demand for educated workers may significantly outstrip the supply." The report estimates that "by 2013, schools would face a shortfall of 686,000 spots" (Baldassare & Hanak, 2005, p. 46).

The report projects that by 2020 California would need 36 percent of its population with some college but instead will have 28 percent. The state will need 39 percent with college degrees but will only have 33 percent. The report states that "the best educated Californians will be among the oldest, as baby boomers head for retirement" (Baldassare & Hanak, 2005, p. 46). But the greatest growth in the state will be among the Latinos, who tend to be "concentrated at younger ages and tend to have low levels of educational attainment" (p. 46).

California's higher education institutions are having difficulty addressing this trend. The higher education participation rates of Latinos in 2005 show that the state is lagging far behind in meeting the needs of this population which consists of large numbers of economically disadvantaged individuals. There were 33,871,000 Californians in 2000. Out of this group there were 10,996,000 Latinos or 32.4 percent of the total population. In 2005, Latinos accounted for 44 percent of school-age children between the ages of five and seventeen. It is estimated that by 2040 Latinos will be 47.8 percent and non-Hispanic Whites will be 30.7 percent of California's population (U.S. Census Bureau, 2000).

Table 7.1 shows in the Fall of 2005 the community colleges should have increased Latino enrollment by 100,000, California

Table 7.1.   Latino Current and Projected Enrollments Based on Percentage of Population in CC, CSU, UC in the Fall of 2005

Category	Community Colleges (CCC)	California State University (CSU)	University of California (UC)
Total Enrollment (Headcount)	1,610,000	337,223	209,080
Current Percentage and Number of Latinos within the Total Enrollment	402,500	67,447	25,089
Latino Enrollment Based on 32.4% (current state population)	521,640	109,260	67,742
Latino Enrollment Based on 44% (current 5–17 year old school enrollment)	708,400	148,378	91,995

Source: California Postsecondary Education Commission (2006).

State University by 40,000, and University of California by 42,000 to just keep pace with current state population trends. More alarming is that the pipeline of students coming through the state's high schools will increase the numbers of eligible Latino students and California's public higher education systems will have to double, and in the case of UC triple, their enrollment to meet this need.

Lack of Sufficient Undergraduate and Graduate Students

Participation of eligible students seeking higher education is not the only challenge facing California higher education. Perhaps even more serious is the continued inability of the systems to

Table 7.2.   Degree Attainment for Major Ethnic Groups (California)

Degree Attainment	Asian/ Pacific Islander	White	Black	American Indian	Latino	Total Number Obtaining Other	Degrees
High School Diploma	11%	42%	7.9%	.8%	38%	.3%	338,967
Bachelor's	22%	52%	5%	.9%	19%	1.1%	112,043
Graduate/ Professional	16%	63%	6%	.7%	13%	1.3%	41,086

Sources: California Department of Education (2004–05) and California Post-secondary Education (2004–05).

graduate sufficient numbers of undergraduate and graduate students commensurate with the state's population needs.

Black, Latino, and American Indian students have significantly fewer bachelor's and graduate/professional degrees than the total population. Latinos, who account for almost 50 percent of school-age children in California, are particularly far behind. Degree attainment for California's major ethnic groups in 2004 as a percentage of their population demonstrates just how far students of color are behind (see Table 7.2).

Of course the K–12 system accounts for much of this failure. Thirty five percent to 50 percent of Blacks and Latinos do not complete high school (Kantorwitz, 2005). Even with these large numbers of non–high school graduates, there still are many disadvantaged Blacks and Latinos who are eligible for the University of California and California State University systems. However, with the rising costs of college and the inability of California higher education institutions to guarantee space, access is denied to eligible disadvantaged students.

Rising Costs of Higher Education and Federal/State Declining Revenues

The rising cost of higher education was discussed by Jennifer Washburn in her 2004 article "The Tuition Crunch: For Low-Income

Students College Is Increasingly Out of Reach." Her article revealed that in "1979 students from the richest 25 percent of American homes were four times as likely to attend college as those from the poorest 25 percent; by 1994 they were ten times as likely.... Since 1980 tuition and related charges have increased at more than twice the rate of inflation, rising by nearly 40 percent in real terms in the past decade alone" (Washburn, 2004, p. 140).

These increases were not offset by the nation's student financial aid system. "In 1975–1976 the maximum federal Pell grant award (for low income students) covered 84 percent of the cost of attendance at a public four-year college; by 1999–2000 it covered only 39 percent. This is part of a broader shift to a system dominated by loans, which has left a generation of students struggling to finance heavy debt. Hardest hit are low-income students, whose numbers are expected to increase dramatically over the next decade. From 1989 to 1999 the average debt of the poorest 25 percent of public-college seniors grew from $7,629 to $12,888 in constant 1999 dollars" (Washburn, 2004, p. 140). The consequences of the average debt forces students to work long hours, attend school part time, and opt for two-year as opposed to four-year programs. All of these factors diminish their chances to obtain a baccalaureate degree. This is particularly troublesome because research demonstrates that the transfer rate for disadvantaged students from two-year to four-year universities and colleges is approximately 10 percent (Washburn, 2004).

The rising cost of higher education and the decline of federal support for low-income students are further exacerbated by the decline of state's resources. The Center for the Study of Education Policy at Illinois State University states that "in most states, higher education is the largest discretionary item in the entire state budget, and the competition is fierce for scarce state tax dollars. State directors report that Medicaid as the key driver to state budgets [and with] increases in K–12 funding and revenue shortfalls due to recession" funding will be even more scarce (Katsinas & Palmer, 2004, p. ii).

Strategies to Address Access and Graduation of Latino Students in the Twenty-First Century

California's state legislative and education leaders are debating what course of action to take over the next twenty-five years. If California higher education is inadequate, what do we replace it with? Should we follow the example of other states such as Texas where the top 10 percent of the students are guaranteed admission and support at the University of Texas at Austin?

The key to addressing the needs of Latino students and the long-term future of the state's economy lies in the development of strategies that are unconventional and that do not follow the classic formula of California higher education. There are new realities in higher education that must be taken into consideration.

Tapping the Resources of Alternative Institutions of Higher Education

California and other states must recognize that they cannot educate the expanding population of students by relying solely on public institutions and delivering education in the same way. States must recognize the fastest growing higher education providers: for-profit, technology-driven institutions such as the University of Phoenix and National University. They deliver BA, MA, and in some cases Ph.D. programs through intensive and short-term courses that accommodate the working adult. They also deliver much of their education online using web technologies, as does the Western Governors University. This approach has much to offer, particularly for students who have to work to support their families.

Transfer and articulation agreements between community colleges, state colleges, and universities with these institutions must be expanded. The free flow of students between these institutions with California public higher education institutions should be guaranteed as students often attend two to four institutions of higher education to complete their baccalaureate degrees.

Establishing Institutions That Specifically Serve the Needs of Latinos

Another strategy is for states to support the development of small semi-private colleges that wish to address the learning needs of the disadvantaged and particular communities. There is a movement in California to build institutions of higher education to specifically serve disadvantaged Latino students. Modeled after the historically Black colleges and universities, these institutions are struggling to establish viable high-quality institutions of higher education that serve the learning needs of second language (English) learners. Most notable is the National Hispanic University (NHU) in San Jose, California. Started in 1980 in a one-room building, the NHU now serves 750 students in east San Jose, has a $25 million capital campaign, owns 7.5 acres of land, and has been accredited by the Western Association of Schools and Colleges. The NHU provides wide access to the disadvantaged. The admission criterion is that a student simply has a high school diploma or general education diploma and possesses a 2.0 grade point average. There are no admission examinations.

The struggle of this tiny institution to gain funding, accreditation, and acceptance in the higher education community has been difficult. But against all odds it has survived and prospered because local corporations saw the potential in an institution that served the learning needs of the fastest growing minority in the Silicon Valley. These corporations realized that barely one percent of the Silicon Valley workforce was Latino and that the public higher education institutions in the area were not graduating Latinos at a sufficient rate to meet their workforce needs.

NHU graduates students with baccalaureates in computer science, liberal studies, and fifth-year teacher credential programs. This institution graduated more Latino teachers in 1999 than did the University of California at Los Angeles. It is a testament to the ability of a small focused institution to make significant gains for specific disadvantaged populations. This is also the case for historically Black colleges and universities who graduate 17 percent of the Black graduates in the nation but whose alumni account for 75 percent of Blacks in law and medical professions (Cruz, 2001).

States needs to invest in these types of alternative institutions and should provide funding for new institutions that have a specific mission to serve the learning needs of Latino students.

Opening the Doors to Foreign Institutions of Higher Education

States should open their doors to foreign institutions of higher education. For example, southwestern states should develop seamless articulation and accreditation agreements with Mexican higher education institutions. Students can study in Mexico or in a Mexican-financed institution located in a border state. This would quickly expand capacity to serve more students and address the need of educated students coming from Mexico to obtain certification in medicine, law, teaching, nursing, and a host of other occupations in the state.

Federal Government's Role: Changes in Title V, Hispanic-Serving Institutions

Supporting special-purpose institutions to meet the needs of the nation's Latino population should be the focus of the federal government's Title V program; Hispanic-Serving Institutions. Created in the 1990s, Title V was established to support institutions of higher education that had a population of 25 percent or more of students who are of Latino descent.

The goal of the legislation was to find a way to fund higher education institutions that were impacted by Latinos and to ensure that access, retention, and graduation of Latinos would increase. There are over 100 institutions of higher education participating in Title V. The majority of these institutions are two-year community colleges with a significant proportion of institutions in Puerto Rico.

Along with the federal strategy to support Hispanic-Serving Institutions (HSIs) came the development of the Hispanic Association of Colleges and Universities (HACU). This organization is comprised of HSIs as full members and non-HSI sister institutions as affiliates. The organization has been responsible for developing partnerships with federal agencies (such as the Department of Agriculture) and private corporations (such as Southwest Airlines) to foster support for HSIs.

So far HSIs have had limited success. Although these institutions enroll Latinos, they still have difficulty in providing greater access, higher retention, and better graduation rates of Latinos in higher education. Many of these institutions enroll Latinos only to have them leave one year later without completing certificate or degree objectives. Unlike special-purpose institutions like the National Hispanic University, HSIs do not have a mission statement to serve the needs of Latinos. They just happen to be located in communities with large Latino populations and are awarded federal funds accordingly and not because they necessarily have the will or vision to serve Latinos.

It is important for HSIs to reevaluate their purpose. I suggest that funding be based on criteria beyond the simple 25 percent enrollment rule. The criteria I believe that would ensure these institutions serve Latinos more effectively are the following:

- Calculate retention and persistence rates of Latinos as a percentage of the total student population attending the college

- Calculate graduation rates of Latinos as a percentage of the total student population of the college

- Include specific mission, vision, and value statements that promote Latino access, retention, and graduation

- Calculate Latino faculty and staff composition as a percentage of total faculty and staff population of the college

- Establish comprehensive partnerships with the K–12 sector to ensure Latino success in secondary education and to ensure students are prepared to succeed in higher education institutions

When revising Title V, it is imperative to rename these institutions Hispanic-Serving Institutions to Hispanic-Graduating Institutions (HGIs). After all, the key is the ability of Latinos to acquire the certificates and degrees to participate in the nation's economy.

Economic Implications

People say why can't Latinos do what the Italians, Irish, and Polish immigrants did? Why can't they simply integrate into the economy and over time accumulate socioeconomic stability? One important difference is that the United States no longer provides the economic foundation to advance. Earlier immigrants could get farm land, manufacturing jobs, and other occupations without a high school diploma and later until the 1950s, with just having a high school diploma.

In today's economy this is impossible. Only 4 percent of the United States' new jobs will be in manufacturing, and inexpensive agricultural land no longer exists in areas where Latinos reside. The Bureau of Labor Statistics (2003) estimates that "employment is expected to increase from 145.6 million to 164.5 million in 2014 or by 13 percent. The 18.9 million jobs that will be added by 2014 will not be evenly distributed across major industrial and occupational groups. Overall the employment in manufacturing will declined by 5.4 percent or 777,000 jobs." The major avenue for economic success is to obtain a baccalaureate degree or occupational certificate. In fact, according to the U.S. Census Bureau, college graduates will earn over $1 million more over their working careers than do people with only high school degrees (Tinto, 2004). This is why institutions of higher education must reform their mission, purpose, and delivery of education to meet the needs of Latinos and the future economy.

Reforming Public Higher Education

I propose four reforms that public higher education needs to make in order to better serve Latinos and other disadvantaged groups.

Delivery of Instruction

Higher education systems must provide flexible delivery of instruction. Changing the rigid sixteen-, seventeen-, or eighteen-week semesters, accepting course work from other sister colleges and universities, giving credit for life experiences, and using problem-based and project-based learning are effective modes of instruction that make learning possible for many learners, particularly the disadvantaged. College courses should be offered at the high school. Accelerated high schools that are placed in college campuses where students can complete a high school diploma and an associate of arts or transfer program credit simultaneously should be encouraged.

Curriculum

In 2004, UCLA's Higher Education Research Institute (Astin, 2004) studied 400,000 high school students and found that 34.3 percent of high school students study six or more hours per week compared to 47 percent in 1987. High school students are entering colleges and universities less prepared. Colleges and universities must revise their freshman and sophomore year offerings to compensate for these deficiencies. English, mathematics, social sciences, and humanities must be able to adopt curricula that emphasize basic skills, composition, critical thinking, and the development of behaviors and attitudes that promote college success.

English as a second language instruction should be incorporated in college courses so that students who are learning English are also learning science, social studies, literature, and art. In this way students whose command of English is deficient do not have to take time-consuming remediation courses prior to enrolling in freshman courses. Team teaching and cocurricular ESL and freshman courses can be facilitated by creating learning communities. These learning communities require block scheduling and students working with each other over a course of a year. The learning community establishes relationships between students, teachers, and counselors that are consistent and operate within the learning requirements of specific subjects.

Finally, the movement for colleges to identify and assess student learning outcomes has much to offer. The key question in the student learning outcome movement is how do you know if the student learned what you taught? It's like the old joke of a teacher who tells a friend, "I taught my students how to whistle." But when the friend asks if he's heard the students whistle, the teacher states, "I said I taught them how to whistle. I didn't say they learned how to whistle."

Student Support Services

Latino and other disadvantaged students require a comprehensive set of support services to ensure their success. First-generation and low-income college students often lack the information, skills, behaviors, and academic preparation to be successful in colleges and universities. States need to further support federal programs such as TRIO that include intensive high school motivational and preparation programs such as Upward Bound. In addition Talent Search programs that identify and inform disadvantaged students about how to apply and secure a place in a college or university need to be expanded. Student support services that provide tutoring, counseling, and supplemental academic instruction are essential to furthering academic and social success on campus.

Technology

Colleges and universities should use technology to teach classes, grade examinations, collect written work, and provide a forum for students to engage each other. The combination of online and face-to-face classroom activity has proven to be effective for many students, particularly students who work, raise families, and have limited time to study during the day. Online courses also allow students to hear lectures or discussions later and to catch points missed in the original learning activity.

Technology will not be effective for Latino students until colleges and universities find ways to provide desktop or laptop computers to all of their students. There are several colleges and universities that have found ways to do this. Leasing, semester computer loans, financial aid funding of computers, and low-cost volume purchasing are some of the avenues colleges and universities can use.

New Revenue Streams to Finance Public Higher Education Reform in California

All of these ideas—supporting alternative institutions, reforming current public higher education, and supporting student participation in higher education—require a bold financial commitment of the state. This is not unlike the commitment California made in 1960 when it decided to invest billions of dollars in higher education. The will and foresight to invest again must be energized.

However, the current fiscal crisis and the inclination not to raise taxes make this commitment difficult to pursue. What then must states do to address the education needs of Latinos?

There are three new revenue streams that states could tap to subsidize these needed changes.

Taxing Free Trade Agreements to Support Educational Development. When the North American Free Trade Agreement (NAFTA) was signed, a group of educators called for a $1.00 tax for every $1,000 of goods and services coming across the border. The idea was that NAFTA must have a companion education engine to support the trade taking place between the United States and Mexico. This tax would ensure that K–12 and higher education institutions could support the citizenry in the southwestern United States and northern Mexico. Residents from both sides of the border breathe the same air, buy the same goods, drink the same water, and attend the same educational institutions.

Create a State Educational Endowment by Selling State Assets. This is not a new idea. Most states own land, warehouses, buildings, and a host of other assets that they can sell and put revenue into an endowment fund. This fund would provide the needed start-up capital to build smaller public and private institutions that are meeting the specific needs of learners. It would target resources to innovative delivery of instruction, curriculum reform, and technology.

Corporate and Individual Tax Credits Earmarked for Education. Corporations should be encouraged to provide support for the state's educational infrastructure. Education trust funds can be supported by employers matching dollar for dollar employee contributions toward these trust funds. The state would provide tax credits to corporations that establish these trust funds. Like Arizona, other states could provide tax credits to individuals who place funds into education trust accounts for their children. These credits can be up to a specified amount such as $825 per couple or $400 per individual. These education trust accounts can only be used to support tuition, fees, and books when a student enters an accredited college or university.

Conclusion

Latinos will be the majority by 2040 in many southwestern states, but the states' higher education systems are not prepared to serve their educational needs. Policy and planning in many states inadequately address the K–12 and higher education needs of the future's largest citizenry. What are the public policy needs of this burgeoning population?

Unfortunately higher education institutions are not asking that question. They believe that if they give more of the same to Latinos, they will succeed. This is not the case. We need bold initiatives in institutional and financial development. We need to get more institutions of higher education committed and funded to meet the education needs of the nation's largest minority. We need to expel old traditions and build new alliances with special-purpose and foreign institutions. We need to change federal policy to ensure that funds going to Hispanic-serving institutions are being used to increase the graduation, retention, and persistence rates of Latinos. We need to find new revenue streams that promote investment over the long term. In short, we need to make a national commitment to the nation's future by investing in Latino higher education.

Part III

A Bright Future
Necesita Un Grito
Fuerte

The need for higher education to change systemically is presented in Chapter Eight, where the focus is on providing leadership that can help to sustain a paradigm shift within Latino communities. Many of the characteristics of current and future Latino communities as described in Chapter Eight by Acevedo are also found in other communities across the United States. The commonalities found in most of our local communities remind us that what is recommended in this book as worthwhile for Latinos in higher education is also beneficial to the United States as a whole. Leadership, vision and planning, education, economic development, and technology are societal factors nurtured in higher education and transmitted to graduates. In Chapter Eight, Acevedo points out that the value of getting a higher education is becoming ever more important, and the stakes of not acquiring an advanced education keep getting higher, not just for individuals but for entire communities and generations.

Because the stakes keep going up, not just for individuals but entire communities as well, Gomez in Chapter Nine states that Latino leaders have come to the conclusion that a bold and ambitious plan is long past due. To try to capture the magnitude of the new plan, we christened this new plan *un grito fuerte*, in honor of the Catholic priest, Father Miguel Hidalgo at Dolores, Mexico, who sounded the bell for independence on September 16, 1810, from Spain's rule. *Un grito fuerte* as described in Chapter Nine demonstrates the need for revolutionary changes in the practices of higher education.

In keeping with the theme of a creating a brighter future, Haro in Chapter Ten points out what few Latino parents and students know, yet the power elite do: not all college degrees are equal. To earn a degree from a private liberal arts college or from an Ivy League campus opens the door to corporate board rooms and public office, where policy decisions are made that affect the lives of Latinos and other populations. College-educated Latinos have a strong propensity to return to their communities and provide public service. Thus, Chapter Ten speaks not so much to change in institutions as to changing the perceptions of Latino parents and students, as well as those involved in college recruitment, so that more talented Latino students can enter into these elite higher education institutions.

8

The Stakes Keep Going Up
Sustaining Latino Communities

Baltazar Arispe y Acevedo Jr.

The economic development of Mexican Americans is grounded in the very military, political, and international law that made them "Americans." In order to understand their present and future roles, it is imperative that a context be developed and delineated so that a framework is available to guide future research. The central theme of this chapter is the emerging challenges and opportunities that the Hispanic community must be prepared to respond to if it is to assume and maintain a presence in the nation's and the global economy. The issues of concern here will be delineated within the context of a proposed "Hispanic Development Helix for a Sustainable Community Model." This model presents several variables (streams) which are proposed as essential to the continued sustainability and viability of this ethnic group in the United States. For the purpose of this dialogue, sustainability is defined by principles and models used in the study of environments and ecosystems. Hargroves and Smith (2005) provide the most succinct definition of sustainability: "progress that genuinely sustains and improves economic, social and environmental well-being with no major trade-offs, locally and globally, now and in the future" (pp. 46–47).

This chapter will also put forth the most current data to substantiate these variables, and several public policy considerations will be proposed as guides for action by this community's leadership.

The diverse ethnic cohorts that compose the "Hispanic community" create a challenge to researchers who are attempting to describe the social status or advancement of an evolving and dynamic community. Most of the research, conducted prior to the mid-1990s, usually focused on Mexican Americans who constituted over 90 percent of the population of these communities. Data from the 2000 census as analyzed by Robles (2005) show that the United States' Hispanic communities are now more geographically dispersed and ethnically diverse and also include an increasing number of Hispanics of non-Mexican origin. Still, a majority of the Mexican American population resides in the five southwestern states of Texas, California, Arizona, New Mexico, and Colorado. While acknowledging the diversity within the nation's Hispanic community, the focus of this chapter will be on Mexican Americans who reside in these southwestern states.

A description of the social development of Hispanics, within a twenty-first century context, must be anchored to international relations between Mexico and the United States going back to the eighteenth century. This chapter will address the conditions of Hispanic Americans in a broad sense and, when data dictates, specific cohorts whose experiences may be unique or impacted by dynamics which are still emerging due to circumstances driven by international law, migration, political participation, or education and economic development.

Historical and Social Context

Zuniga and Hernandez-Leon (2005) reinforced the historical roots of the Mexican Americans in the Southwest by their observation that "the presence of Mexican origin communities in the southwest, their culture, lifestyle and economy predate the arrival of Euro Americans, as the names of streets, rivers, cities and states attest" (p. xiii).

The Mexican citizens who were stranded in the southwestern territories ceded to the United States by Mexico through the 1848 Treaty of Guadalupe Hidalgo have been involved in transgenerational legal battles with the United States for over 150 years to gain their treaty-based enfranchisement. While this treaty created, in essence, the Mexican American, it also, according to Zuniga and Hernández-Leon (2005), failed to impede the movement of people and actually set off migratory flows between Mexico and the United States which, they contend, "have remained largely uninterrupted" (p. xiv). In 2006, the immigrant issue continued to divide voters during the mid-term national elections.

The newly created Mexican American became what the late Chicano poet Corky Gonzales (1967) referred to as "Joaquin" in his classic poem "Yo Soy Joaquin." These are the descendants of the forsaken Mexicans who remained in the southwestern United States after 1848. Social justice and its corollaries, which are grounded in ethical and moral calls for equity, may have satisfied some of the Hispanic community leaders during the empowerment struggles of the 1960s and 1970s. However, social justice and its expectations of just behavior will no longer bode well for the Hispanic community in the emerging political framework. The social justice orientation may also not be of benefit to the immigrant *familia* of the Mexican Americans as the issue of immigration moves to the front burner in both the United States and Mexico. These perspectives are partially based on David Miller's (1979) description of social justice, which he describes as having some of these essential characteristics:

> Not every state of affairs can properly be described as just or unjust. It must, first of all, involve sentient beings, and paradigmatically it involves beings who are both sentient and rational (I shall not discuss whether talk of the just treatment of animals is literal or merely

metaphorical). It must also be a state of affairs in which at least one of the sentient beings is enjoying a benefit or suffering a burden; if no one is affected in either of these ways, questions of justice cannot arise. It must, thirdly, be a state of affairs which has resulted from the actions of sentient beings, or is at least capable of being changed by such actions. [pp.18–19]

A primary consideration here is that Mexican Americans, like other American ethnic groups, have had to resort to legal means and civil disobedience to challenge and ameliorate socially unjust policies and practices of the majority White Anglo policy brokers and government officials in order to obtain rights and benefits that are due them by international law. As our community has matured, so has its intellectual and knowledge capital. It has also created the means to put forth its social agendas through community-based institutions which address its concerns through lobbying, policy, research, or legal initiatives. Among the best known are the National Council of La Raza (NCLR); the Mexican American Legal Defense and Educational Fund (MALDEF); the Hispanic Association of Colleges and Universities (HACU); the League of United Latin American Citizens (LULAC), and the G.I. Forum. This ethnic cohort has, as a "sentient being," suffered burdens, damages, and impediments to their rightful place without the benefits due them as American citizens.

There is no need here to reiterate the many struggles that Mexican Americans encountered in their efforts to gain acceptance and recognition as part of the American social fabric since before the Texas Revolt or the Mexican War (1812). There is, however, a need to access and review current data to present the emerging status of our community's development by visiting those social indices by which progress is measured by social scientists and policy brokers. These considerations will be addressed within the context of sustainability.

Critical Issues for Developing a Sustainable Hispanic Community

The central theme of this chapter is grounded in the principle of sustainability which, it is proposed, will be a critical link to guide the future development, transformation, and participation of the American Hispanic community in this nation's social mainstream and principally in the economy. Alan Atkisson (Hargroves & Smith, 2005) admonishes leaders in general by his statement that "the challenge of sustainability places greater demands on us than is commonly understood. People often speak of 'balancing' economic, social and environmental needs—as though performing a mere tight-rope act, a skillful stroll above the crowd and the safety-net, was all that was required. But there is no safety net; to fail is to crash. The crowd cannot just watch; all must participate. And we need far more than balance: we need *transformation*, a wave of social, technical and economic innovation that will touch every person, community, company, institution and nation on the Earth" (p. xiii).

Of concern is that the diverse Hispanic communities in this nation, and specifically in the southwestern states, need to be prepared to be competitive so that they may participate in the shaping of various policies and legislative agendas to expand their role and scope with targeted outcomes in politics, economics, leadership, health, education, business, and enterprise development. These are the sectors that Atkisson referred to in his preface to the work of Hargroves and Smith (2005). The globalization of economics as well as tension-bearing issues such as leadership, economic enfranchisement, immigration, and political participation will also require a participatory role in shaping foreign policy that impacts this community's presence beyond this nation's boundaries. The essential ingredient is having a formative and transforming strategy that can be constantly evaluated and modified to accommodate changes in the social environment that impact the "Hispanic Future."

The essential elements of sustainable communities are delineated here in a Hispanic Development Helix for a Sustainable Community Model (Figure 8.1). This model is based on and incorporates some of the elements of the Management Helix for the Sustainable Organization (Sustainability Helix) presented by Hargroves and Smith (2005) in *The Natural Advantage of Nations.* (I found no theoretical constructs within educational research or other social sciences that were appropriate to describe the dynamics evident in a sustainable Hispanic community.) The proposed Hispanic Development Helix for a Sustainable Community Model modifies and expands the theoretical constructs that Hargroves and Smith proposed for sustainable organizations. The similarities are in the "activity streams" which, it is proposed, are the essential elements in the Hispanic community's development, if it is to

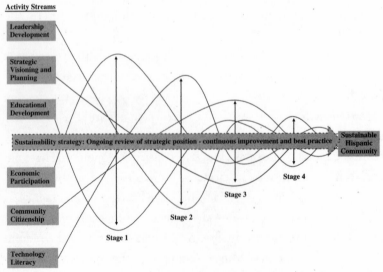

Figure 8.1. Hispanic Development Helix for a Sustainable Community Model

Source: Hargroves and Smith (2005). Adapted with permission of the authors.

compete as a legitimate participant in the United States and global economic mainstream.

This new model represents what Saskia Sassen (2005) refers to as a "type of conceptual architecture" by which one explains social phenomena. The presentation of such a model places an onus on the author to provide, according to Sassen, "its own substantive rationality" (p. 28).

The activity streams, in this model, represent some of the essential elements of the nexus of continuous sustainability for the Hispanic community. It is not meant to be an all-inclusive list as other streams may be identified by the reader or researchers. The activity streams are interwoven at different stages, and the level of interaction and relationship between and among them is displayed as either elongated within a stage and with much space within the dynamic activity, or compressed within a stage. For example, *Stage One* indicates a community that is not very interactive with many gaps to be attended to in terms of sustainable development, while *Stage Four* presents a community that is very interactive and focused on its sustainability. The less interaction, the more space that exists within a stage. The more compression, the greater activity and more interaction is evident among and between the streams within a stage. The challenge, to this community's diverse leadership, is to continuously work to compress the gaps between all streams so that an orientation and commitment to a sustainable future is present. Currently, this ethnic community is becoming a vibrant element in the economic and social mainstream of this nation. The interconnecting thread, which should be dynamic among all stages, represents a strategy that focuses on sustainability which consists of a formative evaluation and which results in continuous improvement efforts based on best practices for all streams. The result is a cadre of Hispanic leaders that sustains itself by being anticipatory, which allows them to understand and analyze emerging social, political, economic, and cultural issues within both the national and global environment and prepare a responsive agenda that works to meet the demands of the future.

The proposed activity streams also provide the substantive rationality that Sassen (2005) contends is necessary for such perspectives. The following activity streams are presented to anchor the central theme of this chapter.

Stream One: Continuous Leadership Development

The roles that the Hispanic leadership assumes will be critical to the continued viability, visibility, and creditability of this community in different policy tiers. The following are the proposed essential elements of the leadership profile that the southwestern Hispanic community needs to subscribe to in order to respond to emerging challenges and opportunities that are becoming more globalized, particularly along the United States/Mexico border:

- There is a need to train a cadre of leaders who are skilled in strong communications. We must train our future leaders to work with diverse groups and to negotiate and meditate as well as reach consensus or compromise as the situation may warrant. The Hispanic leadership must know what Eberly (1994) refers to as "the language of public life [which] is the dialect of the quantifiable, the rational, the scientific and the technical-language of calculation and control ... but also the language that conveys values and meaning" (pp. xiii–xxiii). Future leaders will be challenged more often to convey what it means to be Hispanic in a nation that is becoming more and more diverse. Knowing your roots and "where you came from" will be a guide for the development of policy positions and corresponding action plans.

- The emerging Hispanic leadership must understand the process of public policy and all of its ramifications. The challenge here is to train a representative cross-section of the Hispanic community in the environments where policy originates at all levels of the public, private, and not-for-profit sectors. Of concern here is the need to identify the best practices in those programs that are focused on creating a leadership that understands the role and scope of policy brokering. The focus should also be on creating leaders that are as Rooke and Torbert say (2005) "adept at creating shared visions across different action logics—visions that encourage both personal and organizational transformation" (pp. 67–76).

- Leadership training programs must be directed toward the development of "global citizens" which Kenichi Ohmae (1990) views as an integral component of the global and interlinked economies anchored in strong information technology networks.

- A critical lynchpin to this leadership orientation is a thorough understanding of data and how to acquire, use, and apply it and make it the basis of all policy brokering. Data-free arguments (we are the poor Brown and ignored people of this nation) will no longer suffice. The positions that our leadership takes must be grounded in timely data presented in the technology-based formats that the majority power brokers can understand and respond to.

Gibson, Rhi-Perez, et al. (2003) have provided a leadership model (see Figure 8.2) which has a binational context and which presents several variables that are of value to the stated hypotheses and to the southwestern region where the majority of Mexican Americans reside. This model, which evolved from research in Cameron County, Texas, and Matamoros, Mexico, presents constructs that can be migrated to other southwestern states and

QUALITY OF LIFE
• Inadequate Infrastructure
• High Unemployment & Low Wages
• Inadequate Healthcare
• Increasing Crime

LEADERSHIP
• Foster a Regional
Binational Community
• Leverage Assets
• Open to Innovation & Entrepreneurship

BUSINESS & INDUSTRY
• Emphasize Education & Knowledge Assets
• Invest in Knowledge-Based Industries
• BinationalTechnology Entrepreneurship
& Career Development
• Create Wealth

EDUCATION & TRAINING
• High Drop Out Rates
• Dead End Careers
• Little Post-Secondary Education

Towards Regional
& Binational Decline

Towards Regional
& Binational Prosperity

BUSINESS & INDUSTRY
• Emphasize Land & Physical Assets
• Dependent on Tourism & Service Industries
• Limited Career Growth

EDUCATION & TRAINING
• Enhanced Education Access
• More Graduate Degree Programs
• Research & Development

LEADERSHIP
• Promote Competition
Between Communities
• Colonialism Mentality Which
Resists "Outside" Input

QUALITY OF LIFE
• Infrastructure Serves the Population
• Recruit, Grow, and Retain Talent
• Civic and Social Entrepreneurship
• Innovative Healthcare Systems
• Shared Prosperity

Figure 8.2. Lower Rio Grande Valley: Crossroads for the New Millennium

Source: Gibson, Rhi-Perez, et al. (2003).

regions that are on the United States/Mexico border. This model is directed at the development of the continuous economic capacity of Hispanic communities.

In order for diverse communities to be competitive and sustainable, Gibson, Rhi-Perez, et al. (2003) propose that leadership have the following attributes:

• Fosters the development of a binational community.

• Leverages all assets (economic, educational, technology, facilities, and so on).

• Is open to innovation and entrepreneurship, especially if the focus is the improvement of the economic quality of life of underserved communities.

- Places a strong emphasis on the development of educational and knowledge assets.

- Advocates for the development of a knowledge-based, trained workforce instead of remediation.

- Fosters an educational system with an emphasis on technological literacy as the norm for all students.

- Invests in the creation of wealth and nurtures self-sustaining entrepreneurship. The outcome is a community that is directed at job creation in the private sector instead of in the public sector where one does not own any of the physical inventories, only the intellectual capital that is brought to the task at hand.

- Focuses on the acquisition of more funds and resources for the expansion of graduate and professional programs while increasing the participation in research of Hispanic cohorts in all professional training. (Texas has made strides in the allocation of funding, such as that to support the South Texas Higher Education Plan, which resulted in massive infrastructural development at colleges and universities along the border region from El Paso to Brownsville, and north along the coast to Corpus Christi to San Antonio. Of course this plan did not originate out of the kindness and largess of a White-dominated legislature but rather was a response to legal action under the auspices of the Mexican American Legal Defense and Educational Fund.)

Gibson, Rhi-Perez, et al. (2003) also present several quality of life elements that are the result of sound leadership:

- Infrastructure that serves the population: Economic development of any community must exist within an infrastructure that promotes progress. Infrastructure goes beyond the physical and includes the technological backbone that is necessary to be connected with the global economy.

- The Hispanic community, if it is to have a meaningful economic role, must recruit, grow, and retain talent. One of the greatest challenges is for talented young professionals to be recruited, nurtured, retained, and promoted in their respective careers so they can develop into a leadership core that will serve their community for a significant time.

- The shared prosperity and quality of community health that is present in a region is also seen by Gibson, Rhi-Perez, et al. (2003) as reflecting the investment of leadership in such outcomes.

The downside of an orientation to the leadership elements proposed by Gibson, Rhi-Perez, et al. is essentially negative social regression, such as loss of civil rights, loss of equity, and so on. With the proposed skills in hand and an orientation to economic prosperity, this emerging leadership should be prepared to navigate the labyrinth of the nation's policy maze. The absence of such a focus will be a retreat to the pre–civil rights era.

Stream Two: Strategic Visioning and Planning

The Hispanic community's assumption of significant roles in the economic mainstream of the nation must be guided by both a strategic vision and a corresponding plan. The Hispanic community must be prepared to first of all recognize opportunity and then become fully engaged in achieving goals. Anything less is serendipity. The preparation component of this model is grounded in a leadership that has a vision for the community. Vision is defined according to Schermerhorn (2002) as "having a clear sense of the future that one hopes to create or achieve in order to improve upon the present state of affairs" (p. 337).

Schermerhorn goes on to state that "visionary leadership brings to the situation a clear sense of the future and an understanding of how to get there" (p. 338). The strategic planning process is the road map to the future that will be a key element of this community's development as a viable participant in the national and international economies and all related social and political opportunities. The foundation for this strategic planning process is a clear sense of the present and the continuous tracking and benchmarking of the barriers that need to be overcome to achieve the targeted vision.

A continuing requirement for the Hispanic leadership will be an ongoing review and benchmarking of the status quo of the Hispanic community in the southwestern states. These data should serve as the baseline to gauge the civic participation status of the targeted communities in making progress that is measured by how certain barriers or impediments are dissolved by constructive participation in city council meetings, school board meetings, and so on. This leadership must be in a proactive mode. The onus will be on leadership development initiatives to prepare leaders that know how to access, analyze, and apply data to make strategic decisions for situations that are emerging rather than to react to events as they are transpiring. This difference in orientation is what Dixit and Nalebuff (1991) refer to as "strategic insight" which occurs when we know how to evaluate "other people's action that tell us something about what they know, and we should use such information to guide our own actions" (p. 24).

Stream Three: Educational Development

The continuing educational development of the Hispanic community as measured by secondary education graduation rates, enrollment in postsecondary institutions, and graduation rates from these same colleges and universities must be a priority.

The educational status of Mexican Americans is another benchmark that must be evaluated by this community's emerging leadership. Frank Newman (1985) believed that the participation of minorities in the professional life of the country was contingent on whether they made progress in "entering programs of higher education that lead to the professional and managerial life of the nation" (pp. 89–95). In order to have college-ready high school graduates, there must be high retention and graduation rates of Mexican American students from public education.

Hargroves and Smith (2005) also address this essential element of development when they make reference to UNESCO's 1997 statement that "the power of universities to educate provides humanity's best hope and most effective means to achieve sustainable development" (p. 436). Hargroves and Smith go on to say that "universities also prepare most of the world's managers, decision-makers and teachers and also play significant roles in national and global economies themselves. They train the next generation of teachers who will in turn teach millions, and they train society's designers, whether they be engineers, industrial designers or architects. It is crucial that universities understand the benefits of whole system design for sustainability in order to help achieve sustainable development" (p. 437).

Robles (2005) showed that nationally Hispanics still lag behind in the educational achievement. The data, which uses the twenty-five-year-old adult as the baseline cohort, show that in 2002, 27 percent of Hispanics had less than a ninth grade education and 16 percent were still in the ninth to twelfth grade. The fact that only 45.9 percent of this population has a high school diploma, compared to nearly 60 percent for the balance of the population, diminishes its capacity for enrollment in postsecondary education. Only 11.1 percent of this cohort has a bachelor's degree while the balance of the population is at 29.4 percent. The low percentage of bachelor's degrees diminishes the pool of applicants that can be considered for enrollment in graduate or professional schools which are essential to the development of an ethnic professional community as asserted by Frank Newman (1985).

In Texas the need to expand the participation of underrepresented ethnic groups was addressed by the state legislature in 2001 by its passage of the Texas Higher Education Plan, also known as Closing the Gaps by 2015 (Texas Higher Education Coordinating Board, 2004b). One of the core goals of this plan was to increase enrollments in state institutions of higher education by 500,000 by 2015. Of this targeted goal, Hispanics are supposed to account for 341,600. The rationale, as cited in the law, for such a goal was that "At present, a large gap exists among racial/ethnic groups in both enrollment and graduation from the state's colleges and universities. Groups with the lowest enrollment and graduation rates will constitute a larger proportion of the Texas population. If this gap is not closed, Texas will have proportionately fewer college graduates" (pp. 2–3).

It is unfortunate that the achievement of the targeted college and university enrollment goals for Mexican Americans have been consistently lagging for the past four years. The most recent 2004 annual report data (Texas Higher Education Coordinating Board, 2004b) show that Hispanic enrollment in Texas has a shortfall of 20,500 students. There is no data that show the attrition rates of all students in Texas higher education institutions and more specifically that of Mexican Americans. It is unrealistic to issue a report that appears to present a population that would be maintaining a constant enrollment trend. The success indicators fail to account for how Texas institutions of higher education are replenishing the numbers of students who drop-out. According to the Texas Higher Education Coordinating Board (2004b), Hispanics and African Americans in Texas represent 55 percent of the population but only 36 percent of the enrollment in institutions of higher education.

The failure of the Texas Closing the Gaps plan is that it is not linked to the closure of the gaps in other social indices and does not consider how K–12 public schools can close the gaps. College readiness cannot be measured solely on the basis of academic achievement and not consider access to quality health care, poor nutrition, substandard housing, and social isolation, such as residing in *colonias* along the United States/Mexico border. To do so assumes that higher education functions in a parallel universe to the other social enterprises. An adherence to such a public policy orientation is both short-sighted and ill-advised in that it leads to short-term solutions rather than continued sustainable ones that all societies need in their educational development.

Stream Four: Economic Participation

The issue of the economic viability of Hispanics, as measured by median earnings, has been addressed extensively by Robles (2005). The national data show that 53.8 percent of non-Hispanic Whites compared to 26.3 percent of Hispanics earn $35,000 per year (Robles 2005). Data provided by Acevedo, Rodriguez, and de los Reyes (2004) for the state of Texas (Figure 8.3) confirm Robles's data at the state level. The discrepancy is more pronounced since median earnings from the balance of the state of Texas are being compared to the poorest counties in the state in the Rio Grande Valley which has a 90 percent population of Mexican Americans. The poorest counties in Texas, with the highest concentration of Mexican Americans, will consistently have annual earnings that are 30 to 45 percent less than the balance of the state. The data is significant since it is from a state which has the second largest concentration of Hispanics both in the Southwest and in the nation after California.

The Texas data varies very little from that presented by Anderson, Holzer, and Lane (2005) in their compilation of national statistics as presented in Table 8.1.

Hispanics and African Americans continue to lag behind the Whites and Asians in mean earnings on a national level. The data show that Hispanic males have mean earnings that are $23,364 less

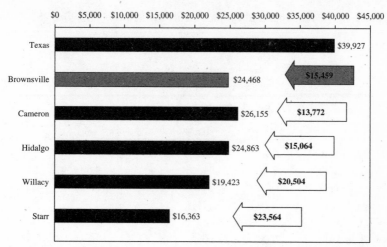

Figure 8.3. Median Texas Household Income—Regional Comparison: 1999.

Source: Acevedo, Rodriguez, and de los Reyes (2004).

than White males and $11,680 less than the $34,781 annual mean for all workers. Hispanic males have the lowest wage earnings of all male ethnic cohorts. Hispanic females have mean annual earnings of $20,414 which is $14,367 less than the mean annual wages for all workers. The annual mean average for White, Asian, and African American females is $27,147 or $6,733 more than the mean annual wages for Hispanic females, which makes them the lowest wage earners for all cohorts regardless of gender. The Texas data reaffirms that this condition is as pronounced in one of the five states which Mexican Americans are the majority ethnic population.

Stream Five: Community Citizenship

The Hispanic community must be, as described by Eberly (1994), "citizens that are socially engaged" (p. xiii). Also, they need to be economically global in understanding. The assumption of these two roles: an American citizenry while also being a global citizen

Table 8.1.   Earnings and Employment, by Demographic Group

	Fraction in Each Group Who Are Low Earners	Mean of Total Annual Earnings	Quarters of Employment	Full Quarters of Employment	Number of Employment
All workers	0.08	$34,781	11.37	9.89	1.91
By race-ethnicity and gender					
White females	0.1	28,732	11.43	10.07	1.8
Black females	0.12	23,948	11.42	9.87	2.11
Asian females	0.08	28,762	11.39	10.07	1.88
Hispanic females	0.16	20,414	11.3	9.79	1.92
White males	0.03	46,465	11.35	9.9	1.85
Black males	0.09	27,868	11.26	9.37	2.43
Asian males	0.07	34,524	11.26	9.7	1.99
Hispanic males	0.09	23,101	11.21	9.37	2.3
By age					
25 to 34	0.08	27,640	11.28	9.47	2.22
35 to 44	0.07	37,036	11.4	10.03	1.81
45 to 54	0.07	41,970	11.44	10.31	1.6
By place of birth					
Foreign-born	0.1	29,144	11.28	9.75	1.98
U.S.-born	0.07	35,912	11.38	9.92	1.9

Source: Andersson, Holzer, and Lane (2005). Used with permission of the publisher.

will require a balancing act that has not been common practice not only among Hispanics but among Americans in general.

On one side are the traditional "ethnic-political roles" that guided our community during its empowerment and civil disobedience in the 1960s and 1970s. On the flip side are the demands of having to attend to local and regional agendas which are engulfed in the global economies that are now commonplace in the "new world." The definition of an engaged Hispanic citizenry is that it is temporal and its values are now part of the ever-changing diverse communities that populate the United States. An example is how the Hispanic community's immigration policy position affects its corresponding positions on localized workforce and economic development initiatives when it is trying to make a distinction between "native-born Hispanics" and "immigrant Hispanics." In some instances these two competing communities are vying for the same meager economic pie. This tension will continue to test the mettle of this community.

It is important that the Hispanic community define its role within the context of the emerging diverse ethnic environments that will determine and dictate the social policy roles that it will act on. Will Hispanics let their ethnicity or their social, political, and economic issues define their agendas? Being an engaged citizenry will mean that the Hispanic leadership must work for collaborative and shared public policies while ensuring that it does not compromise the welfare of its developing community.

Nowhere is such a collaborative agenda more evident than in the recent May 2005 mayoral election in Los Angeles, where Antonio Villaraigosa, a Hispanic city council member, forged a coalition of African Americans and other ethnic communities to win the mayor's race, an office which has not been occupied by an individual of Mexican origin for over one hundred years. The focus was on issues that impacted all communities rather than just the Mexican American community.

The mayoral victory of Antonio Villaraigosa resulted in a national media blitz to redefine and reassess the political capital of Hispanic communities. It seems that demography equates to political and social power when an ethnic minority candidate achieves a top position. Demographics have no political currency, but rather consider the development of what *Newsweek* (Campos-Flores, 2005) refers to as "the fashioning of multi-ethnic alliances" (p. 25), which may yet tell the real political tale. *Newsweek* and *Time* labeled the 1970s as the Decade of the Hispanic. The resulting growth in this community population from 1990 to 2000, as enumerated by the 2000 Census, again resulted in media frenzy and the Hispanic community's assertion that sheer population growth equated to political power.

The reality of the demographic data is that the Hispanic community is fairly young with an average age of less than twenty-seven years and that while it is the largest ethnic group with a population of 44.3 million, it still makes up only 14 percent of the total population of the nation. Just these two facts should give us pause to think about the political currency of the Hispanic demography. The prevailing questions, which should lead to immediate action, are: (1) How much of this population is eligible to vote? (2) How much of this population is registered to vote? and (3) How much of those registered to vote actually voted in the most recent elections regardless of whether these were on the municipal, state, or national level?

Stream Six: Technology Literacy

A core challenge to the Hispanic community will be to build its capacity to first acquire and then to maintain technological skills to anchor its transformation, accommodate the ever-changing global economy, and participate in government which is the lynchpin for public policy.

A key variable that will impact the participatory citizenship roles of Hispanics is that of access to timely information. Historically, government and policy-setting bodies controlled access to data sources. Ohmae (1990) describes this shifting dynamic: "in the past, there were inefficiencies—some purposeful, some not—in the flow of information around the world. New technologies are eliminating those inefficiencies and, with them, the opportunity for a kind of top-down information arbitrage, that is, the ability of a government to benefit itself or powerful special interests at the expense of the people by following policies that would never win their support, if they had unfettered access to all relevant information" (p. 18). The World Wide Web, through the Internet, has leveled the playing field of information access and will become a portal to new public policy strategies.

The use of the Internet, as a political organizing and communications tool, was most evident during the recent 2004 presidential campaigns in the United States. The challenge, will be for the Hispanic community to reclaim its technology heritage, which predated the arrival of Spain to the "New World," and again become "high-tech Aztecs" or technology-literate Mejicanos. A corresponding task is learning the difference between data and its application and also which data has social and economic currency. Knowing these distinctions will make the difference in how information technologies are used to effect change in the quality of life of the American Hispanic community. Don Tapscott (1996) provides some cautionary aspects to the metamorphic nature of technology when he states that, "Reengineering theorists to date have also missed the broader implications of the IT-enabled transformation of business on virtually every other aspect of human work and social life. Huge issues need to be tackled-from quality of work life, retraining, and lifelong learning for the new economy, the changing nature of work, and the end of the career as we know it, the danger of the haves and the have-nots society, all the way to the fundamental changes in the nature of workings of government, the democratic process and democracy itself" (pp. 28–29).

Information technology is part and parcel of everyday social, political, economic, cultural, and educational development. Hispanics must attend to technology in their development while concurrently working on remaining social issues that still linger.

Conclusion

The role that Mexican Americans have in the American and global economy is one which must be considered within a broad context. It can be analyzed within a multiple element context, such as the proposed Hispanic Development Helix for a Sustainable

Community Model. I have suggested elements or streams here and others, yet to emerge, are still in need of research. All too often we stay in our comfort zone and attempt to explain existing social phenomena in terms of immigration, workforce development, political participation, and such only as they relate to our research field. That is a mistake because in doing so we fail to attend to the holistic issues of development, such as higher education, or come after our sometime silo orientation to explain social events.

The proposed Hispanic Development Helix for a Sustainable Community Model is an attempt to go beyond out-dated gender and ethnic models that were generated by White scholars in the twentieth century and which have little use in explaining the Hispanic social experience. Higher education must play a key role in shaping the character of Latino communities by helping to prepare Hispanic leaders, who in turn, will form a more informed and actively engaged community.

9

Old Promises, Contemporary Goals, and Future Dreams
Time for a Bold Plan

Manuel N. Gomez

If when a child is graduated from high school that child is motivated to learn more about self and the world, then I would say that schooling has achieved its overarching purpose.... When I say "motivated to learn" I refer to that individual's curiosity about his or her interests and talents and where and how they can be tested and exploited in a world not of their own making but a world they know they have to comprehend. And that should be as true for the student who is not college bound as it is for those who are.... School is a place a very young child enters with awe, curiosities, expectations, questions, and the desire to feel competent and recognized, and that young child should have personal characteristics when he or she finishes formal schooling. For those characteristics to be extinguished, to go underground, to get expressed primarily in fantasy is to impoverish a lifetime.

Sarason (1995), p. 134

For all my years in academic administration and educational partnership work with K–12 schools, when someone asks me to define the essence of my commitment to educational change, Sarason's quote sums it up more eloquently than I could. Sarason is not just writing about claiming and sustaining a student's attention and intellectual curiosity; he has captured the symbiotic relationship between school and student, the almost ethereal exchanges that occur, and which center on learning as a lifelong, life-enriching activity, and on the student as the center of that process. His profoundly student-centered paradigm is a natural extension of John Dewey's notion that progressive education "requires ... a philosophy of education based upon a philosophy of experience" because the school is fundamentally a social institution (Dewey, 1964, p. 226).

Although much educational reform talk and programming have proceeded from the (sometimes unspoken) understanding that education is a social endeavor, with societal implications, I think we have often felt defeated by the magnitude and complexity of the dynamics that both operate in and seem imposed on the process of schooling. Conflicting, even contradictory, agendas, political shape-shifting, theoretical evolution, and commingling social priorities present a winding and sometimes treacherous landscape for radically minded reformers and change agents to traverse. I think this is part of the reason I am drawn to Sarason's deceptively simple (but not simplistic) formula for school success; it is comprehensive but pristine, and it is very much focused on the student as a way to comprehend the structure and purpose of the system as a whole.

We can talk all we want about the educational pipeline or interinstitutional collaboration or the politics of educational change, but in the end, we need to stay focused on the idea that the sweeping changes we keep talking about and pointing toward are, at some fundamental level, the culmination of countless moments in which individual students have the opportunity and the motivation to learn and then learn some more. I think that sometimes when we use rhetoric about student-centered outreach and school change, we do so with a somewhat abstracted view of students as part of the overall politics of educational reform—as future voters, as economic producers, and as agents of democracy. But these are still individual students who are working their way through homerooms and classrooms and substitute teachers and peer pressures and family obligations—students whose educational experiences are shaped by the quality of the interactions they have with teachers and parents and counselors, with textbooks and tests. We would be wise to remember that at this juncture in our national educational development we need to personalize the student experience more, in school and in our own work and reform planning.

Many of us who ultimately pursued careers that encompass educational reform efforts had very defining individual experiences in school—some negative and some positive. Those of us who went to school in the 1950s and 1960s, and whose first language was Spanish and not English, remember being punished every time we forgot to lead with English in a classroom or even on a school playground. Many of us who came of age in the 1960s and went to college during the height of the Chicano Movement and the Vietnam War protests developed a deep sense of distrust for the "system," with which we still struggle today, even though some of us are now ensconced in that very infrastructure we railed against when we were younger. But many of us who remain active in educational change initiatives and the pursuit for social justice had some very important formative educational experiences that were positively motivating, or we would not have had the incentive to keep going in school and earning the credentials to be educators and reformers, and to dedicate our own careers to "those vividly foreign kids" who are still perceived as in need of "reform" by the assimilative machine of public education—what Joel Spring calls "the sorting machine" (Spring, 1976).

My own fork in the road was carved out by a counselor in high school who kept a sharp eye on me, even, and perhaps especially, when I had stopped watching out for myself. First she helped me get a full scholarship to an Ivy League university, but unbeknownst to her, my early experiences following my parents around cold Colorado fields digging for sugar beets made me retreat from the idea of ever going to a cold climate again. And with my family finally settled in California, I felt even less incentive to go east, and I had no realistic understanding of the magnitude of that opportunity. So then, when many counselors would have written me off as ungrateful, this woman pulled me back into the system and got me into a northern California university, which was a thorny but ultimately successful transition into higher education for a kid who came out of sunny Santa Ana, California, and whose educational experiences had been circumscribed by both class schedules and crop picking schedules. And the fact that this counselor was able to adjust her own expectations for my educational success, to recognize that my path might not be one flanked by ivy, was exactly the kind of support and direction I needed to remain engaged in school and in the democratic ideals of public education that now circumscribe the part of my life that is still lived in school.

My own experiences have clearly shaped my choices and my path, especially my move into a position where I am involved in trying to effect change rather than being the object of change. But the institutions in which I have found myself have clearly played a part in my own development, both as a person and as an educator. On the one hand, my most negative early experiences definitely helped shape my view of public education, and they still keep my passion for educational change percolating at a very personal level. But my ability to negotiate the system as an advocate for change comes in part from my educational immersion in the very values and practices I would like to see changed. It is a balance that I keep reminding myself of, one that requires a sharp eye on both the rebel and the educator sides of myself and the system, if I am to productively use the tension these two sides generate, and effectively direct the sparks emitted from the sometimes grinding friction between them.

It is a balance I have become keen in observing in my colleagues, that we are all struggling to nurture both aspects of ourselves—rebel and mediator—and I have to remind myself that we all worked our way through the labyrinthine structures of the educational system in order to put these competing forces to powerful use on behalf of change. Sitting and looking around that big conference table in Austin, Texas, I was struck by the accumulation of professional experience and the resonance of patient authority in so many of the voices that come from years of struggle and mediating conflicts inside the "system" of education. How many rebels hide behind the polish and the civilized manner when we discussed the need for a new *Grito*? And as we sat in contemplation of the next revolution, we did not necessarily betray our awareness that not all revolutions lead to change, let alone desired change.

I bring all this up neither in lament or celebration, but simply as an extension of my earlier formulation of schooling as a confluence of individuals and circumstances including students, faculty, administrators, parents, critics, and other educators. For in the same way that student learning is shaped by a cooperative collision of circumstances, experiences, and interactions, so is the work of educators shaped by that same strange alchemy, whether our work coheres in theoretical contemplation of the system or in direct intervention and interaction in specific institutions. The experiences and struggles we have had, the relationships we have built and evolved over the years, the institutions we have worked and studied in, the unique perspectives that form the sum of our experiences, and the influence of those who have come before us, have all helped shape our work in significant and perhaps underappreciated ways. We are very astute in recognizing the influence of individual circumstances on student learning; as far back as the 1930s, George I. Sánchez was advocating the consideration of environment over heredity in the use of tests to measure achievement and aptitude (López & Samora, 1977). We have, however, been slower to recognize the way that the evolution of individual educators, outside of those whom we study and revere as important figures of influence, contribute to the overall state of the educational system and the academic progress of students.

And yet at the same time, we recognize the profound importance of institutional culture in the process of educational change and the need to cultivate alliances and cooperative relationships among individuals, institutions, and systems. This paradox (when you consider the fact that institutions necessarily subordinate the individual to the collective identity of the organization) has created an unusual dynamic in the language and work of educational reform, a dynamic that promotes innovation and novelty but at the same time insists on the entrenched and persistent nature of certain "problems" that seem to elude resolution. This tension between a tenacious faith in the spirit of innovative solutions and seemingly endemic problems in the system that appear to have the resistance of the most virulent epidemic fosters a situation wherein the problems themselves become almost a singular focus of analysis in the hopes of finally unlocking *the key* to a cure. I use the language of disease deliberately here in reflection of the organic character of much educational reform language and the systemic nature of the problems we seem to encounter over and over again.

We also seem to track over the same ground, again and again, positing, parsing, and laying bare the conditions of our educational institutions and our society, at some level recognizing the continuity of these conditions, but at the same time searching for a new way of looking at them, a better, more fruitful mode of analysis, perhaps. Take Sánchez's work on bilingual education and aptitude testing from the 1930s, and then take another look at the latest controversy over the SAT, the fallout from No Child Left Behind, and the current debates over the wisdom of high stakes testing and its usefulness in measuring both students and schools. In such circumstances, it is difficult not to become harried or cynical or simply overwhelmed by the persistence of certain social and educational inequities, and the problems that emerge from and lead to such disparities.

But sitting around that table in Austin with all of my *compañeros* in what can sometimes seem a Sisyphean effort—raising the educational bar for Latino students across the entire educational continuum—I was struck by the spirit of optimism that stayed strong over the two days of discussion and planning and exchange. Many of the faces and names at the table represented both leaders and *veteranos* of educational reform, not only for Latino students, but also on behalf of education in general. Although the balance most definitely favored four-year universities, there were representatives of community colleges and secondary school systems as well, and each of us came to the table voluntarily, with nothing more than a common desire to see change take deeper and wider root and to pledge our own cooperative engagement with each other to this end. We all understood that no single individual or organization or institution holds the key to the kinds of changes we all want to see. And we know that strategic change must occur in the schools, the community colleges, the four-year colleges and universities, and even graduate and professional programs. If there are any keys at all, they will be found in recognizing our interdependence and calling upon our wealth of experience and knowledge.

In the midst of our sessions another notion struck me: we have among us resources that match any monetary funding we could hope to collect and expend on behalf of educational change. Our experience, insight, idealism, and passion, the shared wisdom of lessons learned and successes measured, all of it may be housed in a more tailored package these days, but the power of these collective resources should not be underestimated. For we have within us the passion for fundamental change—that idealism forged at some formative point in our education or our careers—along with the perspicuity and comprehensive understanding to negotiate very stubborn practices and institutions. Also, for each of us in that conference room in Austin, there are hundreds and thousands of others, working in schools, colleges, universities, and other organizations and agencies, who have a similar mix of passion and perspective. In other words, we have it all, and it is time to take everything we have and put it to a concerted use, relying primarily on ourselves and on the network of leaders within our communities who share the same basic goal: to raise the level of educational achievement for Latino students, thereby improving the social, political, and economic progress of Latinos across this country. At some level, this sounds so simple as to be superfluous and superficial, a redundancy of the clichés we seem so determined to dismantle. I am certainly not suggesting anything new; in fact, what I am really suggesting is that we have so many of the tools and resources in place, and that instead of pushing farther out toward "innovative" strategies, perhaps we should start by looking more closely at what we already know and begin cultivating the best ideas and practices from that field of knowledge.

We know, for example, that authentic collaboration must exist among those who work in the educational continuum to better serve students. The very real differences in institutional cultures, diverse missions, and differing institutional priorities can create power imbalances among those at the table, and only by acknowledging those differences and unanimously working toward a goal that serves each partner can we create the camaraderie and trust necessary to establish actual working alliances between and among institutions. Further, we know that all colleges and universities are not the same, and neither are all community colleges nor primary and secondary schools. We know that a specific solution that works in one institution might not fit the particular needs and priorities of another. Also we know that local control needs to be balanced with certain overarching tenets. We understand that in the same way it took many generations to get to where we are now, that it will take at least one more generation to foster the kind of change we might collectively call significant, and although we may have our patience tested, we should realize that this really is the work of a lifetime—perhaps of generations.

We know that change occurs best when there is a strong culture of learning in our communities and our institutions. When we keep pace with the changes in our students, it is clear that while not every student wants to be or would be happiest in higher education, each student is entitled to the best education we can provide at every academic and instructional level. We are poignantly aware of the complex and interweaving intersections between society and schooling, and despite the fact that education is still the best way to achieve social mobility, economic well-being, and freedom, it is also among the most scrutinized and contested of our public institutions, influenced from outside and inside by a myriad of intervening forces and factors. All of this we know, and more.

So in the midst of this incredible storehouse of knowledge, wisdom, and experience, I was asked to capture ideas expressed at the meeting to formulate a plan, *un Grito*, for this volume that had its origins in Austin around a conference table and among a group of highly committed, successful, and generous individuals. We talked briefly about a sort of Marshall Plan for education, and it was this idea I was asked to flesh out in this chapter. But upon reflection, I am not so certain the Marshall Plan is the best model for the kind of change to which we aspire now. For one thing, the American political and economic dominance ensured by the Marshall Plan does not reflect the type of equitable partnership we want to foster in public educational reform. And while the notion that economic vitality supports political engagement within our democratic values is worth keeping in mind here, the political underpinnings of the Marshall Plan do not make it an ideal model for a new strategy in our context. The Mexican *El Grito* is closer to what we are aiming for, especially as it embodies not so much a detailed plan for containment but rather an organized strategy or a call for independence, a call from the community for a commitment to change. But there is, of course, the warning about the nature of revolutions to consider here as well.

Yet the nature of the problems reveals a critical need for an imminent strategic initiative. As part of the fastest growing and least formally educated population, Latino students face challenges beyond their control and their making. While their economic power as *consumers* is on the rise (Di Maria, 2006), their opportunities in K–20 education are not growing nearly as quickly. Between 1980 and 2000, Latino representation in higher education grew from a mere 4 percent to only 10 percent (Di Maria, 2006), and by 2020, Latinos are projected to comprise 20 percent of the United States' student population (Mellando & Yochelson, 2006). Currently, 90 percent of Latinos reside in seventeen states (Mellando &Yochelson, 2006), but like other multigenerational immigrants, we are beginning to disperse across the country, including the Midwest (Gilroy, 2006). In California, where Latinos are now a statistical majority but still a political minority, 80 percent of hired agricultural workers are Latino (University of California, 2003), but the state is dead last in the comparative share of undergraduate degrees awarded to Latinos relative to their population rate (Campaign for College Opportunity, 2006). Nationally, Latinos comprise only 3.2 percent of the science and engineering workforce (Mellando & Yochelson, 2006), which makes the rise to a 64.4 percent high school graduation rate even less impressive (Jaschik, 2006). California is, ironically, lower ranked than Mexico in the number of postsecondary degrees and certifications it gives (Stern, 2006).

We dare not miss the irony that while 40 percent of United States science and engineering doctorates are awarded to international students, Latino students who claim the United States as their home are being woefully undereducated, especially in proportion to their overall population, their participation in the American workforce, and their levels of consumer spending. Even more troubling is the fact that the elements of success for Latino students are neither mysterious nor unique: "committed faculty, effective mentors, strong peer support, rigorous and relevant content, financial assistance and effective transition to the job market" (Mellando & Yochelson, 2006). Unfortunately, out of the eight million people in education, only 7 percent are Latino, and most Latinos with advanced degrees end up in business-related fields (Di Maria, 2006). And the higher up the management chain one proceeds, the fewer Latinos there are in positions of authentic power within education. That so many Latinos ultimately end up in business-related fields should be viewed as a resource when it comes time to place students in the job market, but even before that point, we need to be doing more to ensure the educational success of Latino students. As a recent Organization for Economic Cooperation and Development (OECD) report noted, *unlike* low-paying jobs, knowledge-based industries actually thrive with more appropriately skilled workers, doubling the incentive to promote Latino success in higher education (OECD, 2006).

So where does this leave us? In a reform environment rife with plans and programs and strategies and suggestions, my colleagues and I are hesitant to endorse a Marshall Plan type solution, as previously suggested. Fundamentally, we believe that we know what the problems are well enough, and we know the factors necessary for educational success for even our most at-risk students. There are particular programs working successfully in schools, districts, partnerships, and states across the country, and I am less convinced that we need to *innovate* than perhaps we need to give more concentrated and comprehensive attention to what we already have and have done, both inside and outside of education. Our last great economic and educational boon, for example, arrived with the implementation of the GI Bill, a superficially expensive plan that generated seven dollars in economic benefit and return for every one dollar spent, a fitting rate for the seven million veterans who acquired educational benefits through the plan (Humes, 2006). The original GI Plan worked in part because it was a comprehensive strategy aimed at a young population that, if left unsupported, might very well have suffered grave economic and social disadvantages upon returning from military service with no direct assistance. We are again at an economic crossroads in this country, with our middle class shrinking and no strategic solutions in the offing, despite the fact that the middle class is essential both to a democratic society and free market economy. One thing that hasn't changed, though, is that education remains central to the preservation of both an economic middle class and the kind of social mobility essential to democratic stability.

So consider this paper a new *Grito Fuerte*, a new strong call, for a reinvestment in our Latino students and a comprehensive approach to educational reform. Whereas plans can be inflexible and inappropriately uniform, strategies can be adapted and evolving. Where plans can force external agendas, principles provide frameworks and goals. Where plans require schedules, which in turn work against patience, partnerships, by their very nature, require circumspection and deliberative progress to succeed. These summary differences have become more critical, I think, since the drafting of El Plan de Santa Barbara, circa 1960s (Chicano Coordinating Council on Higher Education, 1969).

While by no means comprehensive, the following principles are intended to be foundational, in the sense that they form the basis of the majority of wisdom surrounding the kind of systemic educational reform we discussed at the Austin meeting.

Develop Rhetoric That Is Promise-, Not Problem-Focused

The balance between remaining aware of the complexity of circumstances and influences that shape educational inequities and planning for a more equitable future is a delicate one. I am not suggesting a kindergarten approach to reform planning—a gold star for every gain—but I am suggesting that we do not superimpose more obstacles onto student learning than are already there; that is, that we refrain from projecting our own fears and points of cynicism too completely on those who we seek to serve. As simplistic as it sounds, I do think we need to see students as both connected to the larger social structure (and all of its likely impediments) and as independent of certain outcomes that we anticipate based on our own experiences and the experiences of students of the past. In other words, I think we need to be more proactive and deliberate in carving out a different future for students and for our educational system as a whole.

Maintain a Balance Between External Conditions and Internal Realities

Each institution—K–12 school, community college, university— has its own individual culture and conditions, many, if not most, of which are related to state funding structures, local demographics, and distinct personalities of faculty, staff, and students. We know that rural students often have different educational realities than urban students, and that small schools may function very differently from very large schools. Schools that have greater diversity are different from schools where most students speak English. Whatever universal conclusions we can draw about educational inequity in the United States as a whole are themselves a summation of individual institutions and communities, few of which are serving Latino students well, and most of which are not. No matter how promising a model program or plan may seem, the conditions of the model and the targeted institutions must be compatible for any hope of real success.

Plan Locally and Remain Aware Globally

One of the things a foundation will ask for when contemplating a grant is the potential for a given program to be implemented in other institutions. Consequently, before you have even had a chance to implement at your home institution, you are asked to think about expansion and replication. So already there is a bit of tension between the innovation foundation money can support and the need for institutionalization they want to see in the return on the investment. While many programs right off the bat will have characteristics that can easily be transferred from one institution to another, it is just as true that certain aspects of any initiative will grow and evolve out of peculiar local circumstances and trends. It is also the case that there are many different institutions trying different things that may seem appealing to an institution trying to get a new program started. While there are numerous resources available to those working in their own institutions, my advice, after many years of collaborative work with schools, community colleges, and universities, is to keep the lion's share of your focus on what is happening locally and within your own institution. Certainly a broader view of social trends and the work of other institutions is important, but if you cannot tailor a program based on your local needs and circumstances, all the outside help in the world will not create the conditions for success. I would also caution against trying to draw in too many elements from other programs; staying as simple and basic as possible will allow you to evaluate what is and is not working, and prevent overlap and duplication of services and projects.

Start at the Roots

Start at the roots if you can't get top-down support and participation. I have seen so many laments that programs cannot get started because the highest levels of management are not on board. But I have also seen projects ultimately win the support and participation of those managers and CEOs once a budding project is off the ground. So really, is it always prudent to wait until you get the kind of funding and support from the top to start planning? Obviously, like everything else, it depends. During the 1960s, when many of us were on the other side of the institutional power structure, we felt that the virtue was in the grassroots, in keeping our ambitions high but our focus on the ground level, at least to begin with. I think it is the same for educational change; there are numerous programs that can find their beginnings in some modest first steps, on which you can build and expand and generate enough obvious results to win the support of those at the top of the organizational levels (and at foundations that might not be willing to fund a project the first time around). The challenge of engaging educational leaders in the process of change, despite the fact that many of them already feel overwhelmed by budget cuts and other social and educational pressures, is best won when those seeking the support have already demonstrated their commitment level and a good deal of work has already been accomplished.

Collaborate Within and Along the P–20+ Pipeline

From preschool to postgraduate programs, an authentically cooperative approach to educational change not only focuses that change at the systemic level, but it builds on resources already built into these institutions. Outside of every other guiding principle for educational change, I cannot stress enough the fundamental and radical transformations that are made possible primarily through collaborative work. Beyond all the wisdom of partnership as an antidote to superficial or limited change, the reality of collaborative engagement across institutions promotes the kind of interdependence that allows a simultaneous focus on multiple problems across several institutions. Collaborative theorists speak of "synergy" in describing the multiplicative effect that mutually engaged partners in educational change create, but what is most important about this energy, is the way it actually can propel a project forward, based on nothing more than the support system created by these links among individuals. Regardless of the formality and extent of the collaborative arrangement—whether it be for one content-specific initiative or an entire curricular change, for example—the mere act of bringing together individuals from complementary institutions in authentic dialogue and commitment to mutually beneficial change can create a rapid shift in perspective and energy level among those who were previously committed but perhaps felt isolated in their efforts and goals. Further, the stronger the relationships built, the more that those at the CEO level will feel enticed to lend their support and participation. On the most basic psychological level, more people will join a party that is already crowded.

Recognize the Gains and Build on Them

A seemingly simple sentiment, but one I believe is not always as easily followed, if only because it is difficult to remain patient in the face of such blatant challenges, minimal progress, and growing regressive losses. But one of the core principles in any programmatic success is the ability to identify even small steps forward and foster them gradually. What this means is that evaluation and assessment are built into whatever activities are under way, and at critical points in that assessment process, small gains can be identified and strategizing can take place focused on keeping the momentum. While a strong temptation in programming is to create ever new additions and permutations of a successful element, my suggestion is to think more modestly, to retain the streamlined approach I suggested earlier and to keep things as clear as possible in the planning and implementation process. One of the most difficult things to confront in programming for change is the phenomenon of intersecting elements. Of course there will always be the confluence of circumstances, individuals, and programming elements that will exert a certain force on any initiative, but beyond this is often a highly ambitious desire to program at multiple levels immediately, making it virtually impossible to determine what is and is not working in any given initiative. While sophisticated programming will ultimately occur, if an institution is still at the beginning of the change process, I would suggest collaborative approaches that begin more modestly and build on recognized gains.

Do Not Get Discouraged with Setbacks and Failure

Sometimes what we might otherwise identify as areas of failure indicate the best indications of where to go next. We talk about the need for innovation and experimentation but rarely give ourselves the room to actually experiment, reigning in quickly if something doesn't seem to be working. In the same way that I suggest a more streamlined approach for new programs, I also suggest a high tolerance for "failure," an evaluation and assessment process that looks at how each element is working and how it might be altered or adapted differently for greater success. This tolerance for setback is accompanied by an equally important need for patience and persistence. One of the chief aspects of experimentation is that it requires enough time for the results to materialize. And early results are not necessarily the best indicators of final results, especially as conditions within and across institutions and communities change. Sometimes one of the biggest challenges for educational change efforts to overcome is when endeavors have reached a level of success that wins the notice of those outside the alliance. There is, at that point, a certain pressure to speed up the gains and keep the project static in order to ensure that conditions remain worthy of positive notice. But no program is static in the same way that no student is static, and no lasting, systemic success will be accomplished within the time frame that most educators, legislators, and foundations want it to be—quick! If we could, in the main, become more accustomed to intermediate successes, to small gains and long-range time frames, then I think we would make much more progress over the long haul. But impatience is always so close to our anticipation for change that it is often difficult to separate the healthy desire for progress and the undermining counterforce unleashed by a need to artificially speed up what is necessarily a fluctuating, uneven, and long-term process, or even more accurately, series of processes.

Share the Wealth

Finally, or at least finally for this list—which is itself just a beginning—sharing the wealth is, or should be, a core principle of educational reform efforts. The more we give, the more we gain. By wealth I am not referring to financial resources as I am to human resources and to the wisdom gained from the work done at individual institutions. I realize that I have spoken largely about collaborating at the beginning of the change process and of seeking institutional resources and assistance from those who are natural educational partners. But the same institutional interdependence that makes such collaboration necessary at the outset also makes partnership the ideal mode of sharing vital lessons and information gained with others who are working elsewhere. Although this assistance is inclusive of publishing the results of experimental programming on a "model" basis, it more often means being willing to personally share experiences and knowledge with those at similar institutions and with those who want to establish similar alliances. It means valuing mentorship among educators in the same way we do in terms of students—because the importance and results really are the same. For if it is not already obvious, the core of work on behalf of educational change is the building, fostering, and expanding of relationships, and the building of educational alliances among educators; among students, teachers, and families; among institutional leaders; among educators, community leaders, and legislators. Even though individual students remain at the center of our work, the kind of social network that will ensure their success can only be provided by the sharing of resources, influence, and experience by those of us who wish to be agents of change.

There is something deeply compelling about the anecdotal, the personal, to the American psyche. For all of our talk of melting pots and multiculturalism, we're still deeply moved by the tale of the "I," of witnessing and confessing, of assembling social order from individual experience. Take, for example, a recent story from *Wired* magazine, a profile called "La Vida Robot: How Four Underdogs from the Mean Streets of Phoenix Took on the Best from M.I.T. in the National Underwater BOT Championship" (Davis, 2005). The entire story is encapsulated in the title, and what a story it is: four undocumented immigrant high school students from Arizona whose genius and discipline nab them an incredibly prestigious award (sponsored partially by NASA), but whose undocumented status is keeping them from the funding and in-state residence status necessary to go on to college. And while the story has incited another debate over immigration policies and the aims of public education, at its core, this story remains—for me—a powerful illustration of the way people and circumstances convene to either promote or prohibit individual student achievement. For these four young men—Lorenzo Santillan, Christian Arcega, Oscar Vazquez, and Luis Aranda—are just that, four young men who still have the passion for learning, the intellectual curiosity, and the raw talent for academic success, and who were given the right support to channel those qualities into academic success.

It is tempting to see them as symbols—of beating the odds, of the failure of democracy, of the failure of public policy, of the need for immigration reform, of the plight of Latinos and the poor in the United States, or of the idea that success is attached to the student rather than the school—but I think it would be a mistake to abstract their story too much. For as irresistible as it might seem, as suited to the spirit of Horatio Alger or the ghost of de jure segregation, the mythologization of *La Vida Robot* draws us, once again, into the realm of the student engaged in the process of learning and underserved by a system that is in place supposedly to facilitate that process. And while these four students still struggle to continue their own learning, there are many more out there just like them—students who are U.S. citizens and residents, who can benefit from the vast wealth of human resources available in those of us who have the will and the wherewithal to work together to make that crucial difference. They are both proof it is possible to beat the odds and evidence that those odds are still far too high for our social comfort. Still, we as educators know what works; we know what doesn't. We as change agents have what it takes; we as Latino change agents just need to get other educators to take it all to a new level of commitment and cooperation. *Ajua!*

10

Where Latinos Go to College Matters

Roberto Haro

While the graduation of Latino students from American high schools continues to increase, their participation in higher education lags behind that of other groups (Hernandez, 2004a). The Western Interstate Commission for Higher Education (2005) report that projects the number of high school graduates between 1988 and 2018 is informative and valuable. In the report, among the major underrepresented racial and ethnic groups, the greatest change is occurring in the Hispanic population. For example, between 1994 and 2002, their numbers in American K–12 public schools increased from 4.8 to 9.2 million students. Meanwhile, the public schools across our country are expected to have approximately 1.4 million fewer White students in 2007–2008 (Western Interstate Commission for Higher Education, 2005). American demographers have known about these trends and shared their data and information with anyone willing to listen. Unfortunately, too few leaders in American higher education seriously considered the rapid growth for Latino high school graduates in the United States. In several western and southern states Latino students are, or will soon be, the largest number of high school graduates.

Types of Colleges and Universities

The types of higher education institutions that will be mentioned in this discussion are: two-year community colleges; private four-year liberal arts colleges and universities; regional four-year universities that include state university campuses able to award up to a master's degree; and doctoral-granting research universities that offer professional training. Proprietary schools and technical training colleges are not included here.

The available data indicate that Latino students do not matriculate through the same types of colleges and universities that Asians and Whites do. The majority of Latino students continue to attend public two-year colleges, from which perhaps less than 20 percent transfer to a four-year college or university (Swail, Cabrera, & Lee, 2004). Latino students who do transfer attend mainly publicly supported four-year college and universities. However, the percentage of students transferring from a two-year colleges to a selective public university remains fairly constant in states with the largest populations of Latinos. Latino students' direct access to private four-year colleges and universities and transfer from two-year colleges to a private liberal arts colleges are disappointing (Swail, Cabrera, & Lee, 2004). At the most selective private colleges and universities, the number of Latino students in the entering classes continues to be very limited, and in many cases less than 10 percent of those who apply and are accepted show up for the fall terms (Swail, Cabrera, & Lee, 2004).

Aside from scholars like Patricia Gandara at the University of California at Los Angeles and Ilan Stavans at Amherst College, there is little literature that addresses the advantages for Latinos to attend selective four-year colleges and universities. Gandara's seminal book, *Over the Ivy Walls: The Educational Mobility of Low-Income Chicanos*, indirectly discusses the benefits of attending an Ivy League or selective private university (Gandara, 1995). Most writers and researchers are concerned that more Latino students attend four-year colleges and universities, usually tax supported campuses, and that they be encouraged to continue their education in a professional or graduate program. There is little mentioned about the advantages of attending a selective four-year college or university. Tangible rewards associated with matriculating successfully in a B.A. or B.S. program at a selective college or university include, but are not limited to, smaller class sizes that provide individual attention in and out of the classroom, closer association with faculty, a residential campus that encourages friendships and peer associations that lead to long-lived networks, and early familiarization with technology such as wireless communication and access to the Internet. Regarding the latter point, at many four-year private colleges and universities, every entering student is required to have a new laptop computer. Usually, this is paid for as part of the financial aid packet a student receives. Attending a selective private campus must be an option for Hispanic students considering higher education.

Several factors need to be considered carefully about where Latinos enroll, or do not, at American colleges and universities. The rapid increase in the Hispanic population across this country raises policy concerns in education that require attention. Besides admission, there are the student policy issues of retention and finance among others. Hispanics, the largest minority population in the nation—even though Puerto Ricans living in Puerto Rico are not counted in the Bureau of the Census total for the Hispanic population in the United States (U.S. Census Bureau, 2002)—have as their primary concern educational attainment. As a part of the American population, this minority group is increasing faster in absolute numbers and as a percentage of the total population than any other group. Yet, their limited enrollment and graduation from colleges and universities, especially selective ones in this country, presents some important challenges.

The decision to attend college is not one that comes easily for Latinos, especially when no one from a student's family has ever attended a college or university. Latino students from low-income, immigrant, and single-parent families do not, for the most part, consider attending a four-year institution directly (Tornatzky et al., 2002). The majority of Latino students from the above backgrounds, if they are considering higher education, will, by design or default, attend a local two-year college. And from there too many of them are diverted into terminal programs, find a job, or simply quit, resulting in very limited numbers transferring to four-year institutions (Tornatzky et al., 2002). Attending a community college does, however, resolve several concerns Latino families have regarding their children and higher education. The cost of attending a two-year college in the Southwest is considerably less than the $6,600 plus tuition costs a year to attend a public, regional university (California Postsecondary Education Commission, 2000a). And this assumes the student will continue to live at home. "Going away" to college poses a major challenge for Latino families because of uncertainties parents may harbor about a son, and especially a daughter, leaving the home. The added cost for housing, food, and incidentals can be daunting for low-income families. The College Board estimates that between tuition, fees, room and board, books, and other incidentals, a student attending a regional public university away from home will need a minimum of $12,000 per year (College Board, 2001). For many families making less than $20,000 a year, the cost appears beyond their means, particularly when there are several children at home. Most middle- and upper middle-class families can find ways to budget for this well before a son or daughter enters college. Moreover, most middle-class families can manage taking out a loan to provide the necessary resources for a son or daughter to attend a four-year college. Low-income Latino families do not feel they can afford to pay the price for a child to go away to college and are reluctant to incur any debt to do so, and for good reasons.

Consider, for a moment, the cost of attending a selective four-year college or university. The annual cost to attend a private institution may be a minimum of $30,000 a year. For too many low-income Latino families, $30,000 represents more than what they earn in two or even three years. Consequently, low-income Latino families consider the cost of a four-year education at over $120,000 unattainable. This high cost partially explains why so many Latino men and women attend public two-year colleges.

The accelerating cost of higher education, especially at the selective private four-year colleges and universities, has caused a dual dilemma for low-income Raza and other underrepresented students. Middle-class families are pressuring, individually and collectively, American institutions of higher education to provide non-need–based financial assistance, often under the disguise of "merit scholarships." Many public four-year colleges and universities have acceded to these pressures and shifted financial resources from need-based awards to programs that benefit students from middle-class backgrounds. In states where there are anti-affirmative action statutes or case law that prohibits "preferences" for admissions and financial assistance based on ethnic or racial and gender factors, established middle-class groups profit at the expense of underrepresented students, especially those from low-income families. While Harvard and Princeton have eliminated early admissions to improve student body diversity, it remains to be seen how many other institutions may follow suit.

It is important to mention another duality confronting Latinos as they prepare for and seek access to institutions of higher education. The number of talented underrepresented students qualified to attend a selective four-year college or university is increasing steadily (Schevitz, 2005). Yet, the numbers of Latino students attending selective private four-year colleges and universities is not increasing at a commensurate pace with the expanding pool of high-caliber secondary school graduates. As highly talented Latino students become a larger portion of the traditional college-age cohort (seventeen- to twenty-four-year-olds), most private four-year campuses are not effectively reaching the parents of these high-achieving young men and women. It remains for new studies to document the increasing number of top Latino high school graduates, and the rather static admissions levels of Hispanic students at selective four-year private colleges and universities. Suffice to say that opportunities exist for private campuses to improve their outreach to underrepresented students and their families and increase the number of high-caliber Latinos in their entering classes.

Why Go to College?

There is no national agenda to address the increasing number of Latino students interested in going to college. The "college-going gap" between Whites and minorities has been widely discussed, even by the leaders of selective private colleges (Clayton, 2003). But few scholars and education policy experts have focused attention specifically on why Hispanics need to matriculate and graduate from four-year colleges and selective universities. Georges Vernez and others at the Rand Center for Research on Immigration Policy have investigated the limited educational attainment of Latinos and made some important calculations and projections. Doubling the number of Latinos earning a bachelor's degree yields some impressive benefits for this country, particularly in the areas of Medicare and Social Security (Vernez & Mizell, 2001). That is, by earning more income, people pay more taxes and thus generate a larger national budget.

Attending a Selective College or University

Closely related to the price tag of a four-year degree, which now may take five plus years to complete at a private college or university, is the rationale for attending a four-year college or university, especially if it is a selective institution. Not all institutions provide the same level of educational instruction and opportunities, particularly in fields such as engineering, mathematics, and science. In addition, the arts are prized and highly recognized at numerous selective American private four-year liberal arts colleges and universities. It's a pity so few Hispanic students with creative talent, and their families, know about such institutions and are able to differentiate among campuses and possible choices.

Among middle-class and well-to-do families, there is a common belief that selective private colleges and universities prepare a higher percentage of their graduates for top-rated graduate and professional schools and that they do a better job of teaching, nurturing, and grooming students for success in life and in leadership in our society than most public four-year campuses. Numerous scholars and corporate leaders trace their success in graduate or professional schools and for their accomplishments and achievements in professional careers to their undergraduate experience at a private liberal arts college. There are tangible benefits associated with matriculation at these institutions that are not well known within the Latino community, especially among the lower economic groups. To them all college degrees are equal in value. But the better informed in our society know that some college and university degrees have an added cache. Several factors make enrollment at these institutions a challenge for Latino students and their parents, especially if they are from low-income families (Gloria & Castellanos, 2003). Cost has already been mentioned. However, the limited experiences Hispanics have with private liberal arts colleges present numerous obstacles for them. While the Ivy League campuses, and some of the better-known private colleges in this country, have recruited high-potential Latino students over the years, the numbers have been very small. Early planning and preparation by the student and a substantial commitment is required among low-income families that desire a child to attend a private four-year liberal arts college or university, especially a selective one. Consider the film *Real Women Have Curves* (2002), a story about the culture and family mores a talented Latina from

East Los Angeles had to negotiate in order to attend an Ivy League institution on the east coast. The film succeeded in dramatizing the challenges many Hispanics will encounter when considering access to a selective private campus.

Educational Preparation and Choices

There are some fields of study that pose significant challenges for Latino students and their parents. In the areas of engineering, health sciences, mathematics, and the sciences, the choice of a suitable college or university must also include critical decisions about the program of study for a student as early as elementary school grades four and five! In the *Tomas Rivera Policy Brief* (2003), a critical question is raised: are all colleges equal in terms of preparation for a science or engineering career? The authors of the document respond with a resounding "no." Colleges and universities vary widely in the selectivity of their admissions, faculty reputation, facilities, and research activities, but most Latino families are not sufficiently informed about these critical factors. The colleges and universities, in turn, cannot significantly determine the level and quality of educational attainment by Latino students in mathematics, the sciences, and technology. Several prominent Latino mathematics and science scholars, such as Dr. Eugene Cota-Robles (professor emeritus at the University of California), Dr. Frank Talamantes (science professor at the University of California, Santa Cruz), Dr. Richard Tapia (professor of applied mathematics at Rice University), and Dr. William Vela (mathematics professor at the University of Arizona), to mention but a few, have initiated important programs to help Latinos better prepare for careers in these fields. Their approach is to motivate, mentor, and provide tutorial assistance for Latino students that will prepare them to do well in these demanding disciplines. Mentors from the corporate and professional sectors are essential in informing parents, especially those with little or no knowledge about going to college, about the choices available for their children, and how and when they need to begin preparing them to attend a higher education institution. Leading Latino scientists and scholars, such as Drs. Cota-Robles and Vela, have worked at the National Science Foundation in Washington, D.C., to develop and enhance programs that reach out to Latino parents and their children, and help them realize their dream of going to college and majoring in mathematics, science, or technology.

Institutional Response

With the above in mind, it is important to consider how different higher education institutions may address or reach out to Latinos and other underrepresented groups. The advent of "mass education"—strategies used to provide options for large numbers of students to access and attain a baccalaureate education—has been widely discussed in the professional literature. I need not discuss that topic here other than to relate briefly the strategies used by higher education planners and policy makers to cope with increasing numbers of Latino students and the deleterious effects of these strategies on Raza. The rapid population increases in the United States, especially among the college-age cohorts in the late 1950s and 1960s, compelled many states to expand existing institutions or establish new ones. Funds to do so were appropriated and expended by the different states and by the federal government. The majority of students seeking access to higher education, at that time, were White. Federal and state agencies, therefore, took the necessary steps to enlarge degree programs and faculty, hire staff, and expand or construct new campuses to accommodate the demand. The best example of a state policy document that provided vision and structure to address the above concerns was the California Master Plan for Higher Education. It was a forward-looking document in the 1960s, but the composition of our student populations in the K–12 schools and in the traditional college-age cohort (seventeen- to twenty-five-year-olds) has changed. By the late 1990s and into the foreseeable future, the face of students wanting to go to college is and will be composed of larger and larger numbers of people of color, especially Latinos.

Comparisons by Types of Institutions

To better appreciate the experiences Hispanic students may encounter as they plan to attend a four-year campus, it is important to examine some of the conditions and factors that determine not just the choice of an institution, but successful matriculation. Three types of four-year institutions will be considered: regional four-year colleges and universities that are state supported; state-supported doctoral-granting research universities; and private four-year liberal arts colleges and universities. Community colleges have already been mentioned and discussed only as they relate to matters concerning the four-year colleges. The Ivy League and other highly selective private universities will be mentioned in passing, particularly in the discussion of selective four-year liberal arts institutions.

Regional Publicly Supported Four-Year Institutions

State-supported four-year colleges and universities (the latter often referred to as regional universities) are favored by Latino applicants for education at the baccalaureate level. Enrollment of Hispanics at state-supported institutions as freshman or transfer students from other campuses or two-year colleges continues to be among the highest for all types of four-year institutions. In states with large and expanding Latino populations, such as Arizona, California, Florida, Illinois, New York, and Texas, these institutions continue to attract Latino students for several reasons. Affordable tuition, proximity to the student's home, information from peers, advice from school personnel, and, in a few cases, open enrollment that allows admission with minimum requirements are factors that may influence the decision to attend such a campus. However, too few of these institutions provide Latinos and other underrepresented students with adequate information on the academic preparation needed and core subjects that must be mastered before completing high school, such as advanced algebra and precalculus, biological and physical sciences courses with laboratory work, and English language and literature. Moreover, Latino parents are seldom apprised of the necessary preparation to qualify for and then succeed in a four-year college or university if admitted. Once a student is admitted to a state college or university, limited skills in or lack of exposure to one or more of the core subjects mentioned above will require what is often referred to as "remediation." The availability, let alone the quality, of remediation provided by state colleges and universities varies widely, and in too many cases, the school places the entire burden on a student to understand, pay for, and meet the requirements, with little more than a list of options provided. Unable to satisfy the remediation requirements, too many Latino students are forced to drop out (Nora, 2003). Various scholars, Anglos and Latinos, refer to this as "the revolving door syndrome" for Latino and other underrepresented students (Haro, Rodriguez, & Gonzalez, 1994).

Several factors may explain the posture of faculty and particularly academic support personnel at state colleges and universities toward Latino students, especially those with weaknesses in their high school preparation. Indifference because of overburdened work schedules continues to be a major factor in the limited attention and assistance provided by faculty and support staff to Latino students with educational preparation issues. Other factors involve budget constraints, lack of remediation courses on the campus, and in a few instances, subtle biases toward Hispanics.

What is important to consider in reflecting on the behavior of faculty, support staff, and even middle and senior management personnel at these institutions is the lack of funding to develop and support effective programs to reach parents and their children at critical points in grades five to nine when the student can take appropriate courses and find support services to help her or him overcome any potential problems with core requirements for college. Some regional universities, like California State University at Fullerton (see Chapter Five), not only do an excellent job of reaching out to students and their families in the high schools but have programs and activities to help them matriculate successfully once they are admitted to the university. Unfortunately, comprehensive programs at state colleges and universities like the one at CSU Fullerton are not the norm.

Public Doctoral-Granting Research Universities

A few of the most selective, major research universities have made significant efforts to assist underrepresented students to qualify for and be admitted to the campus, some despite case law or statutes that prohibit the use of preferences for minorities and women. The flagship state university campuses in California (Berkeley), Michigan (Ann Arbor), Texas (Austin), and Washington (Pullman) come to mind. Because of initiatives and legal battles challenging affirmative action, far too many state-supported research universities have done nothing or scaled back what programs they had to attract and retain minority students. At some of the most selective institutions, demand for access has completely outstripped available space. This is particularly troublesome in states with large and rapidly increasing Latino populations. Something else exacerbates this challenge. Far too many Hispanic students attend inner-city and rural schools with restricted sources of funding and less than desirable facilities and instruction through the twelfth grade. Latino students from these schools are not, therefore, as competitive as their Asian and White counterparts living in suburban school districts with above-average financial and human resources to assist them to achieve high levels of academic performance. As an example, the University of California campuses at Berkeley and Los Angeles every year turn away thousands of qualified students with high test scores and 4.0 grade-point averages because of a lack of space. Administrative personnel responsible for the admissions process at these institutions are caught in a serious dilemma, as legal restrictions prohibit them from doing anything "extra" to help underrepresented minorities gain access to the institution. Most faculty attempt to address the limited space at these campuses by "ratcheting up" the entrance requirements. Regardless of what criteria a highly selective campus like Berkeley, Michigan, UCLA, or Washington uses to narrow the pool of qualified students to those "most admissible," a troublesome message is being sent to minority families and students. The perception Hispanic families and students have about entrance requirements at selective research institutions is that they are not welcome. It does not matter whether this perception is right or wrong. All that matters is that too many Latinos believe access to these campuses is unattainable.

The reader needs to consider a critical issue regarding the attendance of Latino students at selective flagship campuses like Berkeley, Michigan, Texas, UCLA, and Washington. There are perhaps twenty to twenty-five research university campuses that provide the largest number of qualified undergraduates access to the leading graduate and professional schools in this country. The above-mentioned research universities are all in the top fifteen or twenty on that list. Many Latino parents, unable to afford the cost of a private four-year college or university for their children, once had an alternative: directing their sons or daughters to campuses like Berkeley, Michigan, Texas, UCLA, and so on. However, the anti-affirmative action initiatives and case law have seriously eroded for Latinos that academic pathway to a selective public university and, from there, access to the best graduate and professional schools. The most selective public research universities continue to be an important pathway to success in graduate education and in one's career. It is a pity that some of them now are, in many cases, difficult if not impossible for Latinos to access (Schevitz, 2005).

Private Liberal Arts Campuses

There is little doubt about the benefits for any talented student in attending a selective private liberal arts college or university, especially if it is a residential campus. A high percentage of graduates of selective liberal arts institutions go on to the top-rated graduate and professional schools in this country. The status associated with matriculation at these institutions is not well known within the Latino community.

Private liberal arts colleges and universities, for the most part, try to recruit a cohesive entering class each year that is consistent with the institution's mission. Therefore, these schools make a conscious effort, especially many of the better ones, to recruit high-potential minority students as part of the entering class each year. The percentage of minorities recruited may vary from college to college. However, the more selective liberal arts campuses generally attempt to admit minorities at anywhere between ten and twenty percent of the total entering class in the fall. While the tuition at these institutions is high compared to most public colleges and universities, these campuses try to offset the cost for qualified students from low-income and underrepresented groups through the use of grants-in-aid, loans, and work study. Some private colleges have sufficient funds to meet almost 90 percent of a low-income student's financial need. A few of the Ivy League campuses, most notably Princeton and Harvard, will find a way to cover the cost for a talented minority student to matriculate at their campus. In California, the state-administered Cal Grant Program actually provides more funds to a student attending a private college than one enrolled at a publicly supported university. The mission and orientation of most private liberal arts colleges is to groom and nurture students, rather than the "benign neglect" associated with mass education at the large state-supported colleges and universities.

To better understand and appreciate the advantage a selective private college provides for its students, consider the conversations I had with three Latina/o graduates of such campuses. I interviewed two women and a man who had graduated from Grinnell College in Iowa, Pomona College in California, and Williams College in Massachusetts. All of them expressed complete satisfaction with their campus of choice. All of them indicated they were well treated at each location.

The Latina who attended Williams indicated the location of the college was isolated from large urban centers. However, the faculty and staff made a conscious effort to make her feel welcome. Moreover, the motivational approach at the college was designed to help her optimize her performance and qualify for one of the top graduate schools in the country. She said, "At first I was intimidated by what they expected of me. However, at the end of the first academic year, I learned that the faculty and my advisors were really interested in me, and pushed me to do better constantly."

During a recent visit to Texas, I interviewed a Latino graduate of Grinnell working in health services. He shared a few experiences about his preparation at the college for graduate study in the health sciences. "People at the college worked with me to build my course of study to match the career path I had selected. I was given several chances to do internships where my course work in biology and chemistry was useful. And the research projects and results of field trips I did in my senior year were sent, along with comments from my faculty mentors, to graduate schools. I was surprised when the graduate school of my choice offered me admission, and a scholarship."

A talented Latina businesswoman from Los Angeles who attended Pomona College said that the support she received from counselors and some of her professors at the college made all the difference in the way her portfolio for graduate school was prepared. "I could not believe how beautiful and well organized it was." Moreover, her writing and mathematical skills were weak when she entered Pomona. But by her senior year, she had been mentored and tutored in both subjects and was able to do very well on both the Graduate Record Exam (GRE) and the graduate management aptitude exams.

The above interviews and comments are but three examples of how some private liberal arts colleges work to nurture and prepare their students for access to graduate and professional schools. The high quality of instruction, mentoring, and individual attention students at selective liberal arts colleges receive has definite payoffs in their professional careers and personal development.

I raise the above examples to dramatize the kind of support and services offered by most liberal arts colleges. The three examples illustrate how private colleges can help Latino students achieve academically and go on to a high-caliber graduate program or professional school. If more Latino middle-class parents were aware of how these colleges assist students to excel academically and to prepare effectively for study in their field of choice, they might consider finding a way for their sons and daughters to seek admission to them, especially if they knew these colleges offer substantial financial support to needy students.

It is important to mention how admissions personnel at graduate programs and professional schools interact with these colleges. The relationship between graduate school recruiters and decision makers and undergraduate campus faculty and staff is critical. The deans and assistant deans responsible for admissions at most top-rated professional schools regularly visit selective colleges and universities. This is part of an established network of contacts that help them identify and recruit talented students. The alumni of professional schools serve as local contacts for their alma mater and interview prospects to provide information about the school, its programs, and the value of its degrees. Too many Latino parents and students are, for the most part, unaware of such liaisons. Staff in the career placement and planning offices at many of the selective undergraduate institutions develop firsthand knowledge of a student's capabilities and potential. They can be invaluable allies and provide critical sources of information about gaining access to important networks.

The Importance of Networks

Aside from a few articles and books that have been written about the value of attending and completing degree programs at selective colleges and universities, little, it seems, has been written specifically for a Latino audience about the intangibles of meeting and knowing the right people (Gandara, 1995). Attending a selective private campus can bring a student into contact with faculty, staff, alumni, and especially peers from influential and well-to-do backgrounds. The parents, siblings, extended family, and friends of peers, many graduates of selective schools themselves, often serve on important boards and commissions and can directly and indirectly influence decisions at the local, state, and national levels. Latino students at these private institutions will, therefore, "rub shoulders" with students who may have direct or indirect ties to important leaders and decisions makers.

Moreover, graduates of highly selective and nationally respected private institutions carry a cache associated with their educational experiences. Eventually, if they attain recognition in their fields or professions, they will be perceived as learned individuals, anointed by their institutions to occupy leadership and high visibility roles because of their credentials and accomplishments. Many are, therefore, considered and then solicited for important jobs and roles at local, regional, and even national levels. If appointed to important boards, committees, and commissions, they are in a position to change attitudes and behaviors among policy and decisions makers. Several older but still important studies describe how critical decisions are made in high-level policy groups and commissions that influence our society. *The Power Elite* by C. Wright Mills (1956) and *The Powers That Be* by G. William Domhoff (1978), along with similar studies, delve into the exchanges and interfaces between leaders from different parts of our society. These leaders, many serving on two or more influential boards and commissions, learn and share from the interactive process which may play a significant role in determining policies and practices that affect our lives. Membership in such "exclusive clubs," now popularly referred to as networking, provides access to key decision makers and leaders, and by extension the opportunity to share and exchange pertinent data and information with others. Consequently, when matters involving the Latino population surface as topics for discussion, or perhaps an item on the agenda of a major board or commission, Latinos can speak for the Latino population! The limited number of Latinos attaining senior leadership roles in major corporate, governmental, and labor groups, with even fewer in philanthropy and higher education, does not provide sufficiently informed input on critical matters germane to this minority population and by extension the larger society as well. Therefore, when the opportunities arrive to examine carefully matters that affect Hispanics, a Latino may not be available to speak authoritatively on such concerns. The reality is that more Latinos need to be represented among the power elite in the United States. This continues to be a sore point for the Hispanic communities in this country and a limitation in decision making wherever it involves Latinos.

The above is not meant to imply that Latinos who graduate from selective research institutions and regional public four-year universities will be excluded from influential groups and bodies in our society. Hard work and personal achievement often qualifies Latinos and others for recognition and solicitation to serve on key boards and commissions. Yet, because students from different parts of the country come together at highly selective private liberal arts colleges or universities, living together and learning to interact and share their backgrounds with each other, a positive dynamic occurs that will often continue through their adult working and professional lives. Such networks, therefore, we know to be influential. But unless Latinos are involved in a critical part of the process that can position them for recognition, access to such influential circles will be limited and sporadic at best.

Strategies for Achievement

Participation in one or more programs that provide services to students frequently motivates and assists Latinos and other underrepresented groups to attend college, especially selective campuses. I will discuss two programs, although others exist. The Puente Project has been successful because of the attention it pays to Latino concerns and the difficult path students from low-income backgrounds must negotiate. The other program is the Mathematics, Engineering, Science Achievement (MESA) effort.

The Puente Project

The Puente Project is a well structured and organized model that has been very successful in helping students to improve their educational attainment and enter selective public research universities. The Puente (which means bridge in Spanish) Project was initiated over two decades ago at a community college in the San Francisco Bay Area to serve mainly Latino students. Under the capable stewardship of Felix Galaviz and Pat McGrath (both now retired), it expanded to serve a large number of high schools and community colleges in the state. This program has three components: a Puente counselor, a mentoring program, and a two-year college preparatory English class. Puente counselors work closely with students and parents to ensure the students are enrolled in college preparatory courses, making good progress, and that parents have the information needed to support their child's academic success. An employee of Puente called a Community Mentor Liaison (CML) recruits and trains a successful, college-educated mentor from the community to help students and their families. The Puente counselors and mentor are usually Latinos, which is important because they serve as models of accomplishment as well as share common experiences with predominantly Hispanic parents and students.

A significant aspect of the Puente process is the emphasis on writing. A Puente instructor and counselor coordinate the program that includes two English classes essential for skill development and for transfer purposes. The instruction focuses on writing and critical thinking skills. This academic activity develops strong writing skills and moves the student from narrative or personal writing to rigorous academic prose, including analytical, argumentative, and research-based texts. This preparation has been effective in building critical thinking and writing skills students require for succeeding and excelling at a four-year institution, especially a highly selective one.

The value of the Puente Project is twofold. First, it recruits students at the high schools and prepares them to attend college. Second, the preparation and mentoring enable most Puente students to complete a two-year academic program at a community college and transfer to a four-year college or university, often a selective campus. Puente program evaluators found that a significant number of these students, when compared to non-Puente students, completed their education at a four-year campus and earned a bachelor's degree (Moreno, 2002). In the National Postsecondary Education Cooperative (NPEC) report on intervention programs for underrepresented groups, 42 percent of Puente students, versus 24 percent of non-Puente Latinos, transferred to a four-year college or university (Gandara, 2001). Moreover, Puente students tend to do as well as or better academically than regularly admitted students at a four-year campus. The strong college matriculation and graduation rate from a four-year campus, therefore, contributes to the enormous value provided by Puente and the high degree of success it has achieved in preparing Latino students to stay in college and earn a bachelor's degree.

Because such a high percentage of Latino students do attend two-year colleges, where many of them opt out of an academic transfer program, some version of Puente should be a model for replication in geographical areas where Hispanic youths are concentrated. Similar programs should be established in states that have large and well-developed community college systems and an increasing population of Latino youth interested in going to college.

The Mathematics, Engineering, Science Achievement (MESA) Program

The Mathematics, Engineering, Science Achievement (MESA) effort is a complex and effective outreach program with a national scope. Under the capable direction of Michael Aldaco, an assistant vice president of student development and academic services in the University of California Office of the President, MESA builds a culture of academic achievement through a unique combination of diverse partnerships involving all segments of the state's educational pipeline. MESA operates through a series of partnerships which recognize that no single programmatic approach can meet the needs of educationally disadvantaged students. It is fundamentally an academic enhancement and enrichment program using strategies that bring all partners to bear in advancing student success while providing opportunities for the partners to work together as well. It requires all components such as schools, teachers, communities, families, and students to interact with each other in positive and constructive ways. While MESA activities focus on student-centered programs in the schools, there are school-university collaborations, teacher professional development, and extensive operations that involve community colleges and four-year institutions. Family involvement in MESA is critical, such as the Family Saturday Academies, Family Math Nights, and Family Conferences. But the core aspects of this program focus on developing academic skills in mathematics and the sciences and

188 LATINO CHANGE AGENTS IN HIGHER EDUCATION

preparing students in the K–12 schools and at the undergraduate level for careers in engineering, mathematics, science, and technology. Underpinning the success of MESA is its demanding, rigorous academic preparation for students. Under no circumstances should MESA be considered a remedial program.

The intersegmental partnership developed by MESA is successful because of its networking efforts with the University of California, the California State University, community colleges, independent colleges and universities, tribal councils, community organizations, and the private sector. The involvement of industry with MESA is a reflection of how important large corporations such as Hewlett-Packard, SBC, IBM, Intel, Microsoft, and others consider this effort. Most industry leaders familiar with MESA consider it a model program that should be replicated in other parts of the country. In fact, California MESA serves as a model for similar programs which have been established in seven other states and for pilot programs launched recently in three additional states. Latino MESA participants have nothing but praise for its value in helping them gain access to and succeed in engineering, mathematics, science, and technology careers.

Conclusion

This chapter has focused on choices that may be available for Latino parents and students as they consider institutions of higher education. Where a Latino student attends college is crucial, whether the student chooses to pursue a specialized field in the arts, a career in the sciences, or access to top graduate programs and professional schools. The purpose of this discussion is to stretch the view of Latino parents and students when thinking of higher education and the benefits associated with not just earning a bachelor's degree but the added value certain types of institutions provide in the form of important tangibles and intangibles. Yes, there is a general theme throughout this discussion that revolves around elitism. For some, particularly in low-income communities, the term *elitism* has negative connotations. However, our communities, especially the Latino ones, need outstanding leaders. Their academic preparation, experiences, collegial friendships, and participation in valuable networks are high priorities. To encourage our most talented youth to do any less is neither productive nor wise.

In their important book on the long-term consequences of considering race in college and university admissions, Bowen and Bok (1998) reached some important conclusions in their research. While their study focused mainly on African Americans, with a small section on Latinos, an important, valuable outcome of college graduation applies with equal force to Latinos. Bowen and Bok found that underrepresented students, especially those graduating from selective public and private colleges and universities, tended to return to their communities and become active workers to improve conditions there. Many went on to become civic and political leaders, far more than their White counterparts. The preparation of future leaders, groomed and prepared for such roles at selective four-year campuses across this country, is an essential part of helping these communities overcome the numerous challenges in the areas of business, health, housing, education, and state and especially local government. The advantages to local Latino communities increase when Hispanic college graduates return to help improve the quality of life in their *barrios* and *colonias*.

It is critical, therefore, that Latino educators, scholars, and leaders make increased college options a priority within our communities. Different strategies are needed to identify and disseminate reliable information on which Latinos can make informed decisions on the kinds of colleges that may provide the most desirable experience for their children. Latino families must be aware at crucial points in a child's schooling what courses and programs of study are essential for college preparation. And, where possible, Latino families should make every effort to find programs for their children like the Puente Project and MESA. The great African American educator W.E.B. DuBois lobbied tirelessly for the development of the "talented tenth" in the Black community. Without efforts and programs to prepare and educate the top 10 percent of the Black community for leadership and success, DuBois said the conditions for the cultural, economic, political, and social development of African Americans would be slow in coming or compromised. Latinos need to take to heart DuBois's idea of the talented tenth and find ways for Latinos to enter and excel in selective colleges so as to be successful beyond their undergraduate and graduate education.

Part IV

Beginning the Work of Reshaping Higher Education

The two remaining chapters focus on two critical variables—leadership and strategic action—that are necessary (but insufficient by themselves) to start the process of bringing about systemic change in the higher education community. All the contributors to this book are calling for breaking the existing mold, not simply reshaping the exterior, that is, what students see on a daily basis or parents hear about from their children and read about in the college publications. We are writing about core practices and fundamental elements. Latino change agents are convinced that their work needs to focus on changing the cultural frameworks of colleges and structural underpinnings of universities. To be successful, we have learned the hard way over the past forty years, two essentials are prerequisite: (1) leaders with vision of equity, and (2) individuals (not necessarily in identified leadership roles) thinking analytically and comprehensively so they and others can act strategically.

In Chapter Eleven, Ballesteros targets the leadership domain directly. While other chapters discuss the importance of leadership, an experienced and now retired Latino administrator concentrates on it squarely. The chapter sheds light onto three facets of leadership: (1) what leadership qualities Latinos and others should possess, particularly in leading institutions where Latinos are to be served; (2) the challenges faced by Latinos in leadership roles who are simply trying to move the Latino agenda forward, (that is, putting students before the institution); and (3) outlining the Latino change agent skill set, also applicable to any person working for significant institutional change.

In Chapter Twelve, the concluding focus targets the book's title, changing the outdated higher education paradigm not just to accommodate Latinos, but to be compatible with a concurrent societal paradigm shift. In so doing, institutions of higher education will better serve all students. Only recently, mostly from the business and political sectors, have social observers come to describe mega-type forces at play resulting in paradigm shifts in society. A good example is the book, *The World Is Flat* (Friedman, 2005). Consequently, Latino change agents, in working to systemically redesign higher education so that it is much more successful in educating Latinos, are in fact laboring to create a system that works for all students and in the end benefits all of society. Through our struggle for change, we, like other enlightened educators, have concluded that if higher education is to remain true to its societal role and to continue to be the sustaining force for a democratic country, it will have to reengineer itself. In recreating a much more dynamic educational enterprise, one that integrates the diversity factor throughout, higher education will play a vital and necessary function of helping to transform society so all have the opportunity to benefit substantially.

11

Leadership Always Makes a Difference

David Ballesteros

L eadership, or more accurately, the lack of it, has received considerable attention recently, especially in politics, business, and education. Although in this book we are concentrating on leadership for change specifically in higher education, we have much to learn from the business world and other professions. When we discuss leadership in higher education we must consider boards of trustees, top management, academic personnel, student leadership, and employees' unions—all critical stakeholders in the important task of "making significant change."

Although officially retired in 2003 after more than thirty years as a professor and administrator—vice president, dean, and CEO of a branch campus (I also taught ten years in high school which was beneficial to my career in higher education)—I continue to teach part-time as a visiting professor at Universidad del Azuay in Cuenca, Ecuador. My own studies have been in courses in leadership and management, and policy and cross-cultural studies in education.

In this chapter on leadership I write from personal experiences including anecdotes and cultural traits, as well as citing current successful Hispanic leaders. I also outline principles and successful practices on leadership and the qualities of a good leader. From my view, an overall topic of this book is leadership, for example, how to move the change agenda forward so Raza can move ahead in their educational pursuits, be economically stable and successful, and enjoy a good quality of life. I challenge the presidents and CEOs of campuses with a significant number of Latino students to take a participative, inclusive, humanistic approach in their leadership styles in contrast to a mechanistic, structural, *"yo soy el jefe"* (I am the boss) style of leadership. The latter style just does not work well for our population.

Leadership Practices

The late Peter Drucker, an expert on management, who dedicated his long professional career to promoting innovation to the not-for-profit sector, said that the first requirement of leaders is to answer these questions: What is our mission? Who is our customer? What does the customer value? What is our plan? (Drucker, 1999). Ret. Admiral William Owens, when addressing the topic of effective leadership at a meeting of San Diego State University deans in the spring of 1993, said leaders must establish the right agenda, do the right thing, surround themselves with competent and understanding individuals, and finally work smart and hard. Jack Welch, former CEO for General Electric, writes in his book *Winning* (2005) that leaders inspire risk-taking and learning by setting the example. Welch says that too many managers urge their people to try new things without proper delegation or directions and then criticize them when they fail. One of my Harvard professors at the Institute for Educational Management was Lee Bolman. In *Reframing Organizations*, Bolman and Deal (1991) talked about leadership frames: structural, human resources, political, and symbolic. According to Bolman and Deal, most leaders use all four of these frames at one time or another, depending on the particular situation to be resolved. For Hispanics, a positive approach would be the human resources frame where a nurturing approach and cultural understanding enhances aspirations and good rapport. Stephen Robbins, San Diego State University management professor talks about leadership as the ability to influence a group toward the achievement of goals. In his book *Organizational Behavior* (2003), Robbins states that in today's world, leaders are needed to challenge the status quo, to create visions of the future, to share these visions, and to inspire organizational members to want to achieve the visions. Unfortunately, in this day and age, we seem to have a plethora of managers and a dearth of visionaries at a time when we need to systematically change the poor conditions Latinos face in higher education and enact new paradigms.

The Twenty-First Century Leader

Jurgen Schrempp, the chairman at Daimler-Chrysler, is an example of one person making a difference. When he took over in 1995, the company was losing billions of dollars because of bad management decisions and had lost its competitive edge to BMW and Lexus. In a very short time he turned Daimler-Chrysler around by taking creative and aggressive steps in mergers and streamlining operations. Schrempp, along with his successor, Dieter Zetsche, exemplifies the attributes of a leader in the new millennium who works hard and smart and is determined to make things work by inspiring his associates. Another example is Ralph Alvarez, president and chief operating officer of the McDonald's Corporation. He has made McDonald's one of the world's largest fast-food enterprises a success story by promoting diversity, customer service, public relations, healthy and low caloric foods, and awareness of obesity and diabetes, especially among African Americans and Hispanics, without sacrificing profit margins for the corporation. McDonald's Hispanic-owned restaurants generate annual revenues in excess of 1.5 billion dollars. Alvarez's philosophy is that an organization never rests on its laurels and always strives to do better (Alfaro, 2006).

What do leaders do? A summary of a leader's duties include: planning, hiring, personnel evaluation, fundraising, decision making, delegation, motivating, rewarding, public ceremonies, and community involvement. In higher education, CEOs and other top administrators will spend a great deal of time with collective bargaining issues where it takes good negotiating skills to come up with solutions and agreements. From my thirty years of experience, I have compiled a list of twenty competencies for the successful leader in the twenty-first century. These competencies are applicable to leaders of various industries, including CEOs and other high-ranking administrators in higher education. A good leader, especially one at a university that serves a large Latino community, should possess the following competencies and character traits:

Competencies

1. Excellent communication skills—verbal, written, listening
2. Team-based interpersonal skills
3. Knowledge of the process of problem solving
4. Understand and value diversity and interaction with different cultures
5. Commitment and preparation for lifelong learning
6. Technology savvy
7. Conceptual grasp of the sciences, social sciences, and the humanities
8. Appreciation of the fine arts
9. Bilingual-multicultural experience
10. Critical thinking and creative skills
11. Computational skills
12. Basic knowledge of interpreting research
13. Understanding of the political and economic systems

Character Traits

14. Well-traveled in the United States and abroad
15. Ecologically conscious

16. Civil, compassionate, and altruistic
17. Socially responsible
18. Good community and global citizen
19. Ethical
20. Physically fit and drug free

While we might not all possess or adhere to these competencies and character traits, the more we strive to use them, the better leaders we will be in our various administrative settings.

From Disadvantaged to Advantaged

In the twenty-first century, who are the real advantaged people? Since the early 1970s I have been promoting the theme in various journals that a bilingual-bicultural person is advantaged. The term disadvantaged has been used through the years to depict Latinos and other people of color as having problems and to excuse the educational system of wrongdoing. We need our college and university leaders to instill pride in our campus communities, accentuate the value of being multicultural, support course work dealing with multiethnic content, promote exchanges with universities in Spain and Latin America, and be visible in community programs dealing with cross-cultural celebrations. Latinos are very much part of the twenty-first century global society because of our history, culture, and bilingual skills.

From Prune Picker to Vice Chancellor

I have had some successes in academia and ample teaching and administrative experiences at the high school, community college, and university levels. I have also learned a great deal from my mistakes, which I have turned into positives. I thank my parents, the Reverend Leonardo Ballesteros, a Baptist minister for thirty-five years in Tijuana, Baja California, and my mother Rosa Ballesteros, who had to drop out of school in the eighth grade to help her family economically. As is the case with most Latino parents, both of my parents instilled good work ethics and high expectations to succeed in school for all of their eight children. Of the eight of us, two received Ph.D.s, two obtained law degrees, and one was the American Baptist Convention field benefits representative for retired ministers and missionaries in the United States and Puerto Rico. Our summers were usually spent in northern California picking prunes and apricots, which provided extra income during the school year and gave us a sense of money management. Also, doing church work allowed us to develop leadership skills at an early age since there were ample opportunities to speak before audiences and provide services. These opportunities proved valuable in my professional career years later.

There were positive accomplishments during my administrative roles at the various universities, and there were also some negative incidents where overt discrimination was displayed, mainly because some White staff and professors felt that a Hispanic was not qualified to assume a high administrative post; in one incident a welcoming reception was boycotted. In some cases, I found it disappointing that Hispanic faculty and staff took a passive role when I needed their help and found it odd when other ethnic groups played a more supportive role. I do not know whether this can be attributed to my leadership style or if this was part of the *envidia* (envy) that many times occurs among Hispanics. These experiences were part of real life for many Hispanic administrators in the 1970s and 1980s when we were the first Hispanics to hold administrative positions. In the early 1970s at the University of Texas at Austin where I was director of Teacher Corps, there was much resistance in getting Teacher Corps interns (mostly Black and Hispanic) admitted to the graduate school in order for them to obtain their master's degrees. It took a year after the program had started for them to gain admittance. I almost lost my job for being too aggressive, for "fighting too hard," so that the interns could be formally admitted into the graduate school. I can say that my action facilitated the admission of these Teacher Corps interns and opened the doors for many more ethnic minority students into graduate programs. I am also pleased that of the thirty interns, seven went on to earn their doctorate degrees. My leadership tactic was to be persistent and to convince the dean of the graduate school at UT-Austin that it was correct, morally right, and in the best interest of the university to admit these students. In so doing, this episode ultimately became a win-win situation for all parties concerned. Today Hispanics are in top leadership positions in the University of Texas System and endowed chairs in academic departments.

While I was dean and CEO of the San Diego State University, Imperial Valley Campus, an Anglo English professor wanted to have a Chicano student expelled from the university because he felt threatened by the student when he wrote an essay in his creative writing class about an instructor being murdered. The professor felt that the student was "after him." This case became a cause celebre on campus where groups took sides either with the White instructor or the Hispanic student. Considering that the nature of the writing class was to develop critical thinking and writing skills and the student was exercising his freedom of expression, I did not see any physical danger to the instructor. I took the side of the student and had him placed in another English class. The student obtained his degree and the professor is still alive. Part of leadership is not to let perceived racial issues fester too long. It is better to come to a quick but measured decision. In this example, it is easy to become trapped in a lose-lose situation. Siding with the professor would have brought the wrath of more Hispanics on campus; siding with the student would have appeared as favoritism to Hispanics because I was Chicano. Needless to say, the end decision pointed to the facts.

In all my administrative jobs, I have always negotiated an academic appointment with tenure, which is common for most academic administrators, but particularly necessary for Lati-nos since their administrative assignments may be shorter than normal. The benefit often comes from teaching. I love to teach so I have always taught at least one course per year in my academic specialty of cross-cultural studies. This brought me close to students, and inevitably there was a dialogue about the mission and goals of the institution. It is refreshing that students in general are honest about what they think of their campus, regardless of whether it is a two-year, four-year, or graduate institution. If you really want to know your campus, I suggest you teach a class. You will get to know your students better and get a sense of student leadership. In one of my international teaching stints, I had the opportunity and pleasure to have a celebrity in class. This was in Cuenca, Ecuador, at the Universidad del Azuay where I teach the organizational behavior and leadership classes for the MBA program. Jefferson Pérez, who won the gold medal (the only one ever won by Ecuador) for the fast walk in the 1996 Atlanta Olympics, was one of my students. Aside from his academic achievements, Jefferson is an example of hard work and determination that made him an Olympic champion with leadership qualities. I learned much just from listening to him, an essential leadership skill.

Many of my colleagues and I have found it valuable to develop a base of understanding about situational leadership through reading, attendance at workshops, and learning on the job. It is important that Hispanic leaders understand that situational leadership decisions are part of a lifelong learning process; you should not expect to step into an administrative position and know it all. The writings of the leadership experts in the education and business arenas who have been mentioned in this chapter are worth everyone's time.

Who Picks Our Leaders?

We sometimes take for granted the stereotypes or perhaps have become victims of Hispanic myths such as that all Hispanics are Catholics, all Spanish-surnamed individuals are bilingual, all Hispanics are Democrats, all Hispanics drive Chevrolets, all Hispanics are poor administrators and should not be promoted. In my three decades of dealing with institutions of postsecondary education—community colleges, four-year campuses, doctoral-granting universities—I have observed with keen interest who gets ahead among Hispanics: *los altos, blanquitos, y bonitos o los bajos, morenos, y feos* (the tall, light-skinned, and pretty, or the short, dark, and ugly)? Most of the time, it is those who look more White than Latino. To get promoted, do we surrender our cultural armor or stay firm in our beliefs on what is good for la causa? Do the *habladores* (the glib) have a better chance of getting the better positions?

To retain our administrative positions, do we have to think "White"? Are we viewed by other Latinos as "Coconuts"? How aggressive can we be to defend our rights of Raza and still retain our positions? Are we only effective in leading "Brown" institutions or can we be leaders in "White" postsecondary institutions? In my estimation, a leader is a person who has values, *no se dobla* (stays firm), takes risks, has high self-esteem, is decisive, and is not threatened by younger and perhaps more talented Hispanics. Do we spend all of our time lobbying among Raza or do we try to gain support from all parties. Obviously, we need to know who the decision makers are, for example, trustees, regents, executive staff, and so on. Let me try to answer some of the questions posed above.

There is no question in my mind that a leader has to be articulate and have a good public persona. When you are on the short list for an administrative position, ask three or four persons for a mock interview to ensure that you answer potential questions without hesitation and focus on your thoughts. There is no need to disguise your ethnicity and cultural background; be proud of who you are and consider it as an added value to what you bring to the job. You might have to follow a Machiavellian approach during the interview phase and not appear "too Hispanic"; once you obtain

202 LATINO CHANGE AGENTS IN HIGHER EDUCATION

your appointment, do what is right for Raza and everybody else. No matter how much we defend our *gente* (people) we will always have detractors who will label us as *vendidos* (sell-outs). Do what you think is right and do not lose too much sleep. If you are viewed as a fair and ethical person and present the facts, you will be fine; the key is consistency and fairness and not to waiver from day to day. You can be aggressive on the truth without being disagreeable. Hispanics can lead "White" as well as "Brown" institutions of postsecondary education. Our bilingual-bicultural background and our humanistic legacy will be an asset to all campus personnel and students. Do not spend all your time with Raza constituents; level with them and tell them that to strengthen Hispanic causes you must gain support from many groups both inside and outside the institution.

We must defend our rich cultural legacy and still provide effective leadership. The Spanish-speaking world has a humanistic legacy, men and women like the great Chilean poetess Gabriela Mistral and Spanish short story writer Ana María Matute, both defenders of children's rights; the Cuban poet José Martí who fought for the liberation of his people; the Mexican President Benito Juarez who fostered respect for peoples of the world; the Puerto Rican Eugenio María de Hostos who made great strides for educational advancement of his *compatriotas*; and the Chicano farm leader, César Chávez, who fought for dignity for the field workers. Although the dream of Simon Bolívar of uniting the new Latin American republics in the early nineteenth century was not accomplished, his leadership motto was that in unity there is strength. There is no question in my mind that as the number of Hispanic leaders increases, particularly women (women tend to use a more democratic leadership style), in significant higher education positions nationwide, our educational system will follow a more humanistic path and lead to better relations among our diverse society.

The Need for Advocacy

In the 1980s at an American Association for Higher Education (AAHE) conference, I recall discussing the idea of a Hispanic organization within AAHE versus forming an independent Hispanic organization. In that same decade, the Hispanic Association of Colleges and Universities (HACU) was born to promote the Latino agenda in higher education and to address the need for students, faculty, staff, and administrators. HACU has been an effective organization through the years with very able leaders. One observation: HACU only grants full membership to institutions with a minimum of 25 percent Hispanic enrollment, and this has prevented several doctoral-granting institutions and other universities with significant Hispanic enrollments from becoming full members. For instance, San Diego State University had over 7,000 Latino students in the fall of 2006 but does not meet the 25 percent requirement to become a full HACU member. However, the SDSU branch campus in Imperial Valley with about 700 students does qualify because of a higher percentage of Hispanics. Universities offering graduate programs, particularly doctorates, must play a key leadership role and make a difference as we move to alleviate the shortage of Hispanic faculty. These are the institutions that need to enroll doctoral students who in turn will teach in our colleges and universities. Whether these universities are run by White or Brown persons, it is important that the Latino agenda is on the front burner. HACU will help institutions to hire more Latino faculty and administrators.

At historically Black colleges and universities (HBCUs) we see African Americans at the top helm, whereas in Hispanic-serving institutions (HSIs), this is not necessarily the case. Unfortunately, many of our HSIs are not led by Hispanics. *Por qué?* (Why?) Are Blacks more united in their efforts to obtain the top jobs? Certainly, the Latino population is no longer behind in numbers as shown by the recent population census. Our leadership knows how to play the political game, thus we must work to be successful in obtaining more presidencies and deanships. Speaking of the political game, the successful election of Los Angeles mayor Antonio Villaraigosa certainly took political skills in building consensus and support among the various racial, ethnic, and religious groups. This coalition united people and led to the success of Villaraigosa's triumph.

Leadership: Placing Students First

The Hispanic agenda is to ensure that students at all levels of the educational spectrum receive adequate attention, resources, and inspiration in order to become successful in the twenty-first century. We want the Latino education pipeline to flow adequately without breakage or interruptions. Articulation needs to take place with school principals, directors, college deans, university vice presidents, and presidents so that each educational level understands what is needed for students to be successful. Head Start preschool and early childhood education programs help children adjust better as they enter kindergarten and primary grades. Also essential is a good bilingual base where children can learn content in whatever language is appropriate. Best of all is having teachers who are well prepared, have empathy, and inspire children to succeed by accentuating their skills, multi-intelligences, and creativity. All children bring some assets that can be explored and developed in order to improve their self-esteem. In recent years San Diego State University has signed agreements with students from middle schools in San Diego County, mostly Hispanic, assuring them admission to the university if they and their parents pledge that they will remain in school and keep up good grades. This also includes financial support if they succeed, so students have five or six years to look forward to enrolling at San Diego State. In this case, President Steve Weber of the university made this commitment with the support of his administration. Leadership always makes a difference. At the high school level, it is imperative that university personnel keep close tabs with teachers and counselors to make a seamless transition into higher education. This might be as simple as having an Open House or Parents' Day to visit campus, meet with Latino student leaders, and obtain the necessary information for admissions and other student support services.

When we discuss postsecondary education we need to make sure that there is adequate communication with four- and two-year institutions and that articulation agreements are in place. Most of our Hispanic students attend two-year postsecondary institutions, and it is critical that this liaison be maintained. Unfortunately, the drop-out rate for Hispanic students at community colleges is excessive (and that is true to a large extent with all students). Again, it is critical that community college students and four-year institutions work together and schedule special visitation days and proper orientations for the potential incoming students. Once students are enrolled in four-year campuses, adequate support is needed, such as counseling, mentoring, financial aid, all vital to their retention and success. When we view education from early childhood through university levels we are looking for leaders to facilitate the flow of students from one level to the other, with these students carrying portfolios that include volunteer work and service to the community. We want leaders who are more committed to students than their institutions!

As we all are very much aware, in addition to a lack of sufficient Hispanic administrators in higher education, we also have very few faculty, and those we have many times do not have the right credentials and experiences to obtain tenure-track appointments. In my estimation one of the big problems is that we have so few graduate students pursuing doctoral work. I commend the Hispanic Border Leadership Institute at Arizona State University and other graduate and research universities for assisting Hispanic students in their pursuits of doctoral work. Again, I challenge HACU and other organizations dealing with Hispanic issues to concentrate more in working with doctoral-granting universities to ensure a better pipeline for Hispanics.

Leadership: All Higher Education Levels and Stakeholders

Whether you are a trustee, advisory board member, president, vice president, dean, department chair, or director, you play an important role in advancing the Hispanic agenda. This also should involve those of us who are emerita because of our long affiliation and experiences with postsecondary institutions. We all should be aware that the ultimate product of our institutions is successful and timely student graduation. Whether there is a Hispanic as the president or not, someone must recognize the needs of Hispanic students, staff, and faculty. Community leaders also have a stake in promoting Hispanic leadership, since it will be beneficial to the institution's internal and external constituents.

A few years ago, when I was a dean at San Diego State University (SDSU), the university gathered all the stakeholders—deans, student leaders, community representatives, alumni, faculty senate members, and trustees—for a three-day shared-vision convocation. It provided an opportunity to know each other better as well as to raise questions of mission, direction, student concerns, and academic programs. We spent a lot of time addressing needs of ethnic-minority students, especially Hispanics, which today represent about 21 percent of the student population at SDSU. Needless to say, the coming together of these stakeholders produced a positive direction and a shared vision where all of us were congruent with the mission, goals, and vital programs of the university.

When we talk and discuss direction at higher education institutions, we need to keep in mind a total quality management approach where all units of the campus commit to work together and seek continuous improvement. One small success within an institution is fine, but all administrative units of the campus must be involved if there is going to be institutionalization. Some federal programs like Title III and Title V have proven beneficial to Hispanic-serving institutions since they call for strengthening programs from top to bottom and making sure that after federal funds are exhausted, these programs remain in place using local institutional funds. The bottom line is that we provide access to students and improve retention rates among Hispanic students. Retention will take place by providing adequate academic programs and support services and having a nurturing environment.

Who Is Accountable to Whom?

I have said that one of the good traits of a leader is the ability to involve people in decision making, participatory leadership, although ultimately, the person in charge must make the final decision. What can managers do to improve their decision making? First, analyze the situation and adjust your decision-making style to the criteria your organization values, evaluates, and rewards, and to the cultural environment. Combine rational analysis with intuition; these are not conflicting approaches to decision making. By using both, you can improve your decision-making effectiveness. Try to enhance your creativity; attempt to see problems in new ways.

Accountability involves all of us regardless of our title and position. Presidents and chancellors are accountable to boards. Trustees, if elected, are accountable to the community. Deans are accountable to presidents, and staff is accountable to directors. Colleges and universities are accountable to students. Professors are accountable to students. Accountability ensures that services are rendered effectively and efficiently. Delegation of responsibility or authority by presidents and others is appropriate if the ground rules are established and results can be measured. Delegation without definition is abdication. You must give clear instructions and evaluate on the basis of the assignment. Some managers may want to do everything themselves and not delegate; we might call this micromanagement or lack of trust. If you want to do everything yourself as a leader, you can save the institution a considerable amount of money and eliminate staff. The key point here is that accountability is best used when goals, objectives, and assignments are well described and followed.

Leadership and Ethics

Leadership involves having a vision for institutional direction and guiding team members to take a more participative role in the organization's future. Leadership involves morality, that is, changes contemplated by the leader must not be detrimental to constituents and the organization. Cross-cultural leadership is a must for higher education institutions with a significant number of Latino students. Cross-cultural leadership accounts for various situational factors in which certain styles may be more appropriate, for example, support services for Hispanic students, which many times involve a more personal approach including working with family members.

When mentioning ethics, I always think of Rotary International with which I have been affiliated since 1984 and have served as president of two different clubs. Youth activities are a key function of Rotary International. Soon after its beginning, the 4-Way Test for members was written and adopted to guide the organization, clubs, and members. One of the objectives of Rotary is to encourage and foster high ethical standards in business and professions and the dignifying of each Rotarian's occupation as an opportunity to serve society. The Rotarian 4-Way Test of the things we think, say, or do is:

1. Is it the truth?
2. Is it fair to all concerned?
3. Will it build goodwill and better friendships?
4. Will it be beneficial to all concerned?

These tenets of Rotary International certainly are applicable not only to the business community but to other professions, such as education. Truth, fairness, and creating goodwill and friendships are part of leadership, and the CEO can set this ethical tone. I would encourage the leaders of our Hispanic community to consider membership in a service organization like Rotary because of the many humanitarian projects and youth activities, such as travel abroad and many scholarship awards. Also, it is an avenue to do volunteer work in our part as leaders and membership demonstrates a commitment to improve the lives of people in need in our communities and around the globe.

Leadership Begins at Home

If you as a leader have a family or significant other, count your blessings. Here you have an opportunity to use your leadership skills: participatory leadership, accountability, delegation, feedback, time management, and so forth. If you happen to be the *Mandón* (the bossy one) at home, then very likely you will have the same leadership style at work and that might get you in trouble both at work and at home.

Balancing work and family always has been an issue with leaders that many times leads to separation and divorce, sometimes because of our extreme dedication to our jobs or perhaps an escape from the family situation. As much as we value our administrative positions, we must stay close to the well being of the family.

In addition to awareness of family needs, there must be time for recreation and exercise. Most administrative positions are stressful, and taking care of our bodies is conducive to more mental and physical alertness. This also involves diet and nutrition. Regardless of age, keeping physically fit and maintaining good eating habits will be beneficial to how we feel, act, and perform our job duties.

Make a Difference, Stay Awhile

The average stay for university presidents in the United States is under five years. For Hispanic presidents—and we have very few—that might be even less considering the cross-demands made on them from both Latinos and non-Latinos. Typically the demands from both groups are at odds and place the Latino president in a dilemma. Besides, Hispanics receive keen scrutiny regarding their performances and many times after a three-year stint they are let go.

Some of our Hispanic administrators may use their positions as stepping stones to obtain a more prestigious appointment. There is nothing wrong with this because an advancement may be considered a significant role model position. But many times, when these administrators leave too soon, there is a vacuum left and little is accomplished. If you are going to make a difference, you have to stay a while, roll up your sleeves, and get things done. In my estimation, it takes at least five years to make your mark, accomplish your goals, and establish a relationship with the community and other stakeholders.

A recent article in Hispanic Magazine entitled "Elite Educators: These Hispanics Are Transforming America's Colleges" (Garcia, 2005), mentions several Hispanic presidents, like Modesto Maidique from Florida International University, Ricardo Fernández from Lehman College, Eduardo Padrón from Miami-Dade College, and Max Castillo from the University of Houston-Downtown Campus. These presidents have stayed at their respective campuses, expanded degrees, improved academic programs, added building sites, augmented private funds, and related well to the external community. They are examples of Cubans, Puerto Ricans, and Mexican Americans who represent community colleges, four-year institutions, and research doctoral-granting universities. I would also like to cite Tomás Arciniega for his longevity at California State University at Bakersfield and for his determination to improve the academic status of his campus that did make a difference. In all of these colleges and universities mentioned, although there are many Hispanic students, enrollments include other ethnic minorities and White students; a true leader is able to make a difference with a multicultural population. Many of the private prestigious universities also are positively impacting the education of our Hispanic students, examples are the University of Southern California, the University of Miami, and Brown University.

How Do Change Agents Make a Difference?

Part of leadership is making things happen. Change agents act as catalysts and assume the responsibility for managing change activities. Change agents are in a position to transform the institution by paying close attention to the concerns and developmental needs of their constituents, providing vision and a sense of mission, instilling pride, and gaining respect and trust. These change agents communicate high expectations, stimulate intellectual curiosity, and treat each employee individually. According to Robbins (2003), the options for organizational change generally fall into four categories: structure, technology, physical setting, and people. Changing structure involves making alterations in authority relations, job redesign, and reporting mechanisms. Changing technology involves modifications in the way work is processed and in the methods and equipment used. Changing the physical setting covers altering the space and layout arrangements in the workplace. Changing people refers to changes in employee attitudes, skills, expectations, perceptions, and behavior. Resistance to change usually involves fear of the unknown, keeping habits, wanting security, and protecting economic factors. In dealing with change, consider the following.

What are the characteristics of the environment and campus climate before change is contemplated? Is change a realistic possibility to someone who wants to make a difference? Lasting and meaningful change comes from involving your stakeholders in a shared vision and direction and acquiring the necessary "buy in," not by administrative directives or *pronunciamientos* (fiats).

As change agents, Latino leaders can influence the direction of the institution by pointing out academic programs not relevant to a multicultural environment, working with board members and community leaders, showing charisma, outlining the needed changes, working with other administrators, faculty, and students, and articulating changes that are needed.

Summary and Implications for Hispanic Leaders

Hispanic leaders in higher education are placed in a tenuous position in carrying out their administrative duties. First, they must be the leaders of all constituents. Second, as Latinos, they are also the leaders of la Raza on campus. They are held accountable for their job assignments either by the board of trustees, the president, or the vice president. Latino constituents hold them accountable to promote and protect their interests. Hispanic leaders cannot conduct business in isolation. As part of leadership, political savvy is necessary to move the agenda forward by forming alliances with other movers and shakers for the good of la Raza. In the twenty-first century, leaders must be in tune with the international arena and promote faculty and student exchanges. Concern for individuals using the leadership frame of human resources, that is, people first, is important for the overall good of the campus community. Inspiring high expectations for faculty, staff, and students, having a vision, good ethics, and staying a while in their positions are key elements for success.

In this chapter, I have discussed some key points of leadership, mentioning the humanistic legacy of well-known compatriotas, showing charisma and determination, applying high ethical standards, and serving as a role model to all Raza. I have tried to point out some leadership issues with the purpose of stimulating discussion on what a Hispanic leader should be. I will end by raising questions I hope will encourage even more dialogue at institutions of postsecondary education, at professional conferences, congressional and state hearings, in the private sector, and within our own Hispanic organizations.

What should be the linkage between the Hispanic corporate sector and education?

What programs and special institutes are available to assist Latinos in significant administrative positions and aspiring leaders?

What are some of the strategies to work with governmental officials both at federal and state levels to support programs beneficial to Hispanics?

What steps can be taken to energize a collective leadership of students, faculty, and community to enhance opportunities for Hispanics?

12

Changing Paradigms

As Society Transforms So Must Higher Education

Leonard A. Valverde

The individual is the indispensable agent of change.
You should not be daunted by the magnitude of the
task before you. Your contribution can inspire others,
embolden others who are timid to stand up for the
truth.

Archbishop Desmond Tutu

Throughout this book, the authors, all change agents at some time in their careers, have called for the higher education community to change significantly, so that greater number of Latinos can have access to a college education and in so doing be more successful as the soon-to-be majority student population in the United States. In addition to calling for greater access and better retention, the authors have concluded that the old piecemeal and marginalized approach has had limited success and is now inadequate for today's conditions. Society has drastically changed, and systemic and comprehensive change is now needed within various social institutions. In fact, the call for change is getting louder and coming from many other sectors in society, not just from Latinos and other people of color. Among elected officials across the country, state legislators are concerned with the increasing requests for greater state aid; and at the federal level, the concerns are about the decreasing quality of education and the lack of satisfactory outcomes (Suggs, 2005). University regents and community college trustees hear the constant complaints from students about lack of course offerings and irrelevant curriculum. In the business community, there is concern about inadequately prepared college graduates. In the annual meetings of professional associations, there are more and more speakers and panels that identify the problems mentioned above and other areas where higher education is lagging further behind. As a result, some professional associations have taken action. For example, at the community college level, there is the League for Innovation in the Community College. Eckel and Kezar (2003) in an American Council of Education publication reported on twenty-three four-year institutions as case studies where significant change was tried and chronicled. From the world of foundations, there is the newly established Lumina Foundation for Education in Indiana whose primary focus is on stimulating and seeding programmatic efforts for first-generation, low-income, and racial or ethnic minorities to access and succeed in higher education.

But these mounting calls for higher education to change are generated from surface or overt concerns, and as such, they seem unrelated. However, all these problems are connected and there is an underlying basis or need to change. Fundamentally society's paradigm shift has resulted in an incompatibility between today's societal needs (particularly as seen in the workforce) and the higher education model designed to fit past needs and still in existence today but with minor modifications.

Major Changes in Society

The economy of the United States and other advanced European and Asian countries is based on knowledge. The information age has created instant communication, storage of vast amounts of information, as well as easier access to data. The knowledge economy has accelerated another phenomenon, the expanded service industry. Making up the service industry in part are travel, communication, recreation, entertainment, sports, and all the related activities that go to support these major service markets.

The above societal changes have redirected the economy and workforce preparation of the nation. Similarly the intended outcomes of higher education, particularly at the graduate level, have begun to shift. The value of preserving and learning lessons from the past is secondary to the value of analyzing the dynamics of today so as to help invent the future. The need is no longer to educate a small subset of persons for leadership roles as was the case during the agricultural and industrial age. Since the end of World War II, the need has been to educate the growing middle class or baby boomers. A liberal arts undergraduate education now prepares graduates for employment in the workforce (once the focus of a high school education). With the forthcoming sea change of minorities becoming majorities in the general population (already the case in few large states) along with moving away from the mythical melting pot concept and moving to sustaining ethnic identities and maintaining diversity, higher education campuses can no longer be homogenous with a few "pockets" of minorities. Higher education institutions will need to become multicultural enterprises mirroring the nation and the world. Hence, the reason for discontent, dissatisfaction, and concerns as expressed by students, the world of work, and politicians is basically due to the mismatch between the emerging new societal paradigm and the outdated paradigm of its social agencies, like higher education.

Implications for Higher Education

What does all of the above mean for higher education? First, higher education leaders must recognize that higher education is no longer a privilege for the top ten or twenty percent of high school graduates as defined by academic capability, usually grades and standardized test scores. Higher education must abandon its exclusionary point of view and highly selective entrance examination approach, that is, only the best can get in with a sprinkling of a few students of color to add diversity or meet its social responsibility of representation. This outdated exclusive admission concept and practice has not worked for the general White population as major universities have grown in size, as a review of the freshman retention rates will show. The average freshman retention rate as of 2004 across the country for part-time students was 46.1 percent (National Center for Higher Education Management Systems, 2005). Major universities have had to put in place a growing number of remedial courses to help prepare students for the college course curriculum.

Additionally, colleges and universities must move away from basing their reputations on recruiting and admitting the most academically able high school graduates and then allowing high standards and competition to eliminate up to half the freshman class. The sink or swim view must change to a view of students' having many talents and attributes (such as persistence) which enable them to be successful. Institutions need to adopt this value-added thinking and base their reputations of excellence on the amount of assistance students get from the institution and the amount of growth their students gain while earning their college degrees. Pride should come from having strong organizational holding power, that is, the ability to retain and graduate students, not from failing students who cannot "cut it."

The above illustrations are offered to support the proposition that institutions of higher education must abandon concepts of education that no longer serve society as well as to abandon the outdated band-aid or marginal intervention tactics started in the 1960s to accommodate minority students disadvantaged by the their K–12 schooling and move to systemic and transformation strategies that will suit society's needs. The core of higher education must be redesigned, starting with its view of who it is suppose to serve and how best to fulfill this commitment. Under this new view, diversity is no longer a minor component to show the institution is progressive in its social responsibility, but is a key part of institutional mission and, as such, embedded in its organizational operations. Diversity should not be viewed as an add-on advantage primarily for the student body and secondly for the institution, but should be understood as a part of democratic representation, that is, public education institutions are to provide participation commensurate with the public composition. This is one interpretation of the bedrock principle of democracy. Furthermore, social institutions are to reflect the communities they serve so as to meet their needs. Higher education campuses can no longer be islands unto themselves, different from the larger communities of which they are a part. Thus faculty, staff, and administrators must mirror the new landscape so they can interpret the circumstances accurately.

What Is the New Higher Education Paradigm?

Since education is fundamentally a human enterprise, and since many recent societal changes are the result of population growth and make-up, the new higher education paradigm should revolve around changing institutional culture. By changing culture, I mean working the whole cloth, weaving the entire fabric, not just working on parts of the institution, not just adding on or even substituting new pieces for old ones. An organization's culture is deep-seated and not superficial. To make such changes will require strategic action on the part of leaders in executive roles.

This chapter is not intended to spell out in detail the new paradigm, only to give the prospective change agent better clarity and understanding of what is meant. I believe it is safe to say that change-minded individuals already have a good sense of what needs to be done and why. I have mentioned one institutional cultural change, that is, from selective admission (exclusionary in nature) and all that this entails to greater access via representation (inclusion). Three other cultural institutional changes are called for in higher education: college curriculum, partnerships with minority communities, and partnerships with K–12 schools and two-year colleges will be identified.

College Curriculum

Under the old paradigm where students of color were seen as numerical minorities, higher education's interventions approach was to help the few students of color admitted to feel better about being in a foreign setting. Specifically schools offered a few ethnic studies courses and later created full-blown ethnic studies programs. Typically the scenario across the country has been that Black, Chicano, women's, and Asian studies have been populated by in-kind students. Nonminority students did not see the value or the need in attending such courses since they were not required. These ethnic studies programs were seen by minority students as places where they could identify with and associate with students and faculty of their own kind. Only now are universities considering a multicultural course as an undergraduate lower division requirement of all students, which is too little too late. However, it would be advantageous for all students to know about different cultures, given that the workforce of the future will be competing globally and interacting with people from different cultures.

Associated with curriculum are two other subcomponents: (1) transdisciplinary courses (teams) and (2) instructional delivery. Forward-looking universities are starting all types of bioscience programs, enhancing and enlarging their international studies, and venturing into new global arenas, for example global sustainability. These programmatic start-ups are efforts to keep current or, as institutional faculty like to say, stay on the cutting edge of tomorrow's developments. Similarly in the arena of instructional delivery, not only are computers and student computer labs as important as libraries, but information technology, another example of a new programmatic thrust in higher education, is leading the way in distance learning and promoting asynchronous learning. The success and embracing of this twenty-first century university model is illustrated by the phenomenal growth of the University of Phoenix and the establishment of the Western Governor's University.

Partnerships with Minority Communities

The second cultural change is tied to institutional linkage with external communities. To a large extent, institutions align themselves with major donors, influential politicians, alumni, major corporate employers within the area, or other groups that the institution believes can either help or hurt it. Individuals or groups that represent the interests of persons of color and their communities are typically relegated to secondary or advisory status and, as such, a small number occasionally meet with the institution head. The meetings are more symbolic than substantive in purpose. This relationship will need to change to a more equitable one between the campus and these communities. That is, minority group representation will have to be elevated to the status offered to the above-mentioned traditional groups. An equitable relationship demonstrates a sincere interest on the part of the institution to work on matters of mutual concern and benefit to these communities and the university. As such, the interaction between the two should be proactive and collaborative in order to prevent missteps, negative criticism, corrective action, and so forth.

The other crucial benefit that a public institution will gain from forging a true equitable relationship with minority communities is support. Publicly supported campuses continue to get less and less state aid, and the trend of less financial state support has worsened so much that many public institutions now refer to themselves as publicly assisted instead of publicly supported. This lack of financial support has caused public institutions to act as private institutions in financial matters, such as raising student tuition and fees, fundraising from their alumni and others, and catering to big business and donors. This has worsened the relationship between public institutions and minority communities, mainly because institutions believe that these communities don't have the same influence or resources to help them. However, astute political observers keep reminding the major political parties that their future is tied to capturing a greater share of Hispanic and Black votes, if they wish to win elections. These analyses recognize that the elected political landscape is changing. At the local level, mayors and city council memberships reflect the growing numbers of Hispanics and African Americans. The increased representation of persons of color is happening at the state legislative and at the congressional level as well. Thus, institutions who are gaining larger number of Latino students and thus are acquiring the federal designation of either associate or full Hispanic-serving institutions would do well to establish relationships with minority communities now.

Partnerships with K–12 and Two-Year Colleges

Four-year institutions will need to link much closer with two-year colleges and public K–12 schools. If major comprehensive higher education institutions and land grant institutions are to serve large numbers of Latinos, then better articulation agreements between community colleges and high schools will have to be part of the new paradigm. As is well known, the entry point to higher education for many Latinos and other students of color is open admission campuses, such as community colleges. But we also know that the transfer rates are dismal from these two-year campuses. Similarly, Latinos graduating from underfunded high schools and who are able to get admitted into a four-year university are still insufficiently prepared to successfully handle a college curriculum. Because of this disconnect along the educational pipeline, K–20 councils have begun to spring up in the last fifteen years. It is highly recommended that the "all one system" promoted by Hodgkinson (1999) be part of the new paradigm. Also, for more detailed understanding of P–20 councils and their value in overcoming underrepresentation of ethnic groups in higher education, see the Education Trust report, *Engines of Inequity* (2006).

How to Change the Higher Education Paradigm: Six Strategies

Develop a shared vision. Since the literature about change is replete with the acknowledgment that persons and organizations are naturally inclined against change, big or small, leaders of change should frequently express the need and, more important, stress the benefits gained from change. The best way to do this is to describe a vision of the future, a vision formed with the help of a broad-based campus committee with external representation. The committee's primary task will be to scan the local, state, and national environment. By so doing, the information collected will lead the committee to the same conclusions as the leader and, therefore, a shared vision will develop. It will be much easier to sell a vision to the entire campus community if it is supported by others than just the CEO.

Gain the support of prominent political and community leaders. They will become your allies and motivate those staff and faculty who stand on the sidelines doing nothing to help bring the new vision into being. These political and community leaders will become protectors, shielding you against those who will either behind the scenes or up-front resist the new vision or reject you as the agent of change. Keep in mind the most opportune time to act is at the beginning. Make concerted efforts on many fronts at the start, since the window for change is short. After the newness begins to fade (usually after a year or two), it becomes harder to motivate and engage people.

Place people who support the vision and are necessary to implement changes in key roles. In turn, get them to form a leadership team within their respective areas of responsibility which is responsible for bringing certain parts of the vision to life quickly. Since most academics placed in administrative roles are not trained for such, either informally or formally, put in place assistance so they can understand the dynamics of change. They should learn about gaining much needed buy-in, enlarging participation of staff and faculty, planning, and resource development. If the leadership is solidly behind the vision and if there are pockets of commitment throughout the various university or college units, then momentum will grow. Change breeds change.

Rearrange and restructure units in order to encourage behavioral changes. We have discussed changing the curriculum earlier in this chapter. If ethnic studies are to be more mainline rather than marginal, then their courses will have to be cross-listed with traditional social sciences courses. To foster an interdisciplinary approach, faculty working relationships will need to be rearranged so that student advising information is consistent and course schedules are discussed between and within faculty departments to minimize conflict of course offerings. These types of reorganization will promote more interaction, and new interactions cause new learning. New learning results in different behavior or, in short, organizational change.

As changes come online, start to realign policies to be consistent with the new structures or arrangements, particularly, policies that support and reinforce the changes so as to get sustainability. For example, if diversifying the professional staff and faculty is a central goal, this should be part of the annual review of all personnel. That is, faculty are typically reviewed for merit pay increases based on teaching, research, and service. Diversity should be added to this trilogy. How has the faculty member advanced or contributed to diversity? Has the faculty member recruited students of color or been involved in ethnic or racial community efforts as part of his or her service? Diversity should now become part of faculty's work portfolio and annual evaluation.

Make change visible. Efforts should be made to alter the campus appearance. For example, student unions should display art work that reflects a multicultural society. Banners at different times and in various parts of the campus should reflect diverse holidays, such as commemorating Martin Luther King Jr.'s or Cesar Chavez's birthdays, Cinco de Mayo celebrations, and so on.

In sum, the entire campus should be involved in some form or fashion in systemic change or in bringing about the new vision. If a leader can engender mass participation, the chances of transformational change are greatly enhanced. Change initiated from the top, reinforced by operational teams throughout the campus, and buttressed by external influential persons and groups is a force that few can withstand.

A Few Tactics to Remember

Don't let detractors or naysayers consume your thoughts. Respond to criticism but be selective and measured. Denial is a common phenomenon among conservative institutions, like higher education campuses. Academics rarely see the big picture, since they are too absorbed in their respective academic disciplines. The *Chronicle of Higher Education* (Haney Lopez, 2006) reported that four-year institutions are turning their attention to assisting "older" (code for White) students. These are the type of students they are most familiar with and supposedly which their paradigm matches up with. By refocusing on older students, they extend their avoidance of Latinos and other students of color.

Arm your supporters, particularly the external ones, with information about the change process, so they can help in lowering the internal resistance by campus members. Human nature is for persons to respond to problems. Take for example classroom teachers. When a student becomes disruptive in class, the teacher becomes focused on the child's behavior and if the student continues to be a problem over time, more of the teacher's valuable time is on the problem student than on the entire class. Don't let yourself be distracted by problems. Keep your eye and mind on the prize.

Remain flexible. You can't be precise about your plans and actions. There are no right or wrong answers to bring about change.

Change is more of an art than a science. There will be unknowns and unanticipated consequences. Be reminded that a course of action selected is a strategy. As such, it is thought that the strategy will produce the wanted outcome. But there are no assurances.

Take advantage of unexpected opportunities. Many major donors have developed their wealth not just on hard work, but on innovation. They are more inclined to give to an institution that is more forward-looking than conservative. Generally, the institution does not find these donors; often they coming knocking on the president's door because of something they heard or read in the newspaper about the institution's new direction and desire to serve society better.

Take a calculated risk or learn from your actions. As one goes up the career ladder, there is less and less room for error or mistakes. The higher one goes in the organization, the more one is supposed to know the answers to problems. So it becomes an accepted axiom: Failure is not an option at the top. Yet, as educators we know that students learn from mistakes. In business, improvement comes from modifying and adapting. This way of thinking is a positive way of learning from mistakes. For instance, in the auto industry, engine and car designs are changed to do things that were not functioning adequately in older models, or to keep pace with social changes and desires. Also, over time the plant production of automobiles has changed significantly since Henry Ford created the assembly line.

Higher Education Must Stay True to Its Societal Role and Democratic Purpose

In closing this chapter, it is fitting that we end with the book's overall theme, that is, higher education is responsible for educating individuals who can become active participants in democracy and work towards creating a society predicated on the foundations of justice for all and economic equity.

Out of necessity higher education has started to shift its focus from being the warehouse of past knowledge to being laboratories where science and technology are leading the way to invent the future. As such, higher education leaders are beginning to envision a more dynamic educational process aimed not just at connecting to the current world, but also to helping transform it. Society now expects higher education to mold the future and its citizens.

Throughout the book, all of the contributing authors have argued for reshaping higher education so that it becomes responsive to and provides opportunities for success to the Latino population. But what we know will serve Latinos will also apply to other students of color, including the color White. Specifically, by redesigning higher education comprehensively and deeply, a cultural framework will be created that will serve all students in their pursuit of education. By using the latest technology in the teaching and learning process as well as infusing an interdisciplinary curricula, students will sharpen their intellectual and practical skills.

Finally, while the linkages between higher education and the world of business have become tighter, the same must become the case with ethnic and racial communities and their representatives, whether they be in elected office, advocacy groups, community-based organizations, or religious leaders. Higher education cannot continue to treat future majority groups as marginalized minorities. Equitable relationships with these communities along with equal partnerships with K–12 and community colleges will be necessary to advance the work.

References

Acevedo, B. A., Rodriguez, I., & de los Reyes, O. (2004, May). *The buena vida barrio: A Brownsville transitional neighborhood*. Brownsville, TX: The Cross Border Institute for Regional Development, University of Texas at Brownsville.

Alfaro, C. (2006, June/July). Burgermeister. *Hispanic Trends*, pp. 34–36.

American Council on Education. (2006). *Minorities in higher education: Twenty-second annual status report*. Washington, DC: Author.

American Institutes for Research. (2005, March). *Early college high school initiative evaluation year end report: 2003–2004*. Washington, DC: Author.

Anderson, F., Holzer, H. J., & Lane, J. I. (2005). *Moving up or moving on: Who advances in the low-wage labor market?* New York: Russell Sage Foundation.

Arau, S. (Director), & Arezmendi, Y. (Writer). (2004). *A day without a Mexican*. Mexico: Mar del Plata Film Festival Award.

Arizona Republic, May 17, 2007, P.A8.

Assembly Office. (1986, June). *California 2000: A people in transition—Major issues affecting human resources*. Sacramen to, CA: Assembly office.

Astin, A. (2004). *Cooperative institutional research program: 2004 freshman survey*. Los Angeles: Higher Education Research Institute, University of California.

Baker, E. (2004, December). *Aligning curriculum, standards, and assessments: Fulfilling the promise of school reform.* Los Angeles: University of California, National Center for Research on Evaluation, Standards, and Student Testing.

Baldassare, M., & Hanak, E. (2005). *California 2025: It's your choice.* San Francisco: California Public Policy Institute (http://www.ppic.org/main/publication.asp?i=600).

Baran, B. (2005, November). Planning for California's future: The state's population is growing, aging, and becoming more diverse. *Budget backgrounder.* Sacramento, CA: California Budget Project (http://www.cbp.org/pdfs/2005/0511_demographics.pdf).

Bollinger, L. (2003–4, Winter). "Educational equity and quality: Brown and Rodriguez and their aftermath." *The College Board Review*, 201, pp. 25–29.

Bolman, L. G., & Deal, T. E. (1991). *Reframing organizations: Artistry, choice, and leadership.* San Francisco: Jossey-Bass.

Bowen, W. G., & Bok, D. (1998). *The shape of the river.* Princeton, NJ: Princeton University Press.

Brown v. Board of Education. (1954). 347 U.S. 483 (USSC+)

Bureau of Labor Statistics. (2003). Tomorrow's jobs (http://www.bls.gov/oco/oco2003.htm).

California Department of Education. (2004–05). *Education Data.* California Research Bureau, State Library. Sacramento, CA. (http://www.ed-data.k12.ca.us/accountability/highschoolreports.asp?tab = 3&reportNumber). Web page for reports: www.library.ca.gov/html/statseg2a.cfm

California Postsecondary Education Commission. (2000a). *College cost report: 1999, series B.* Sacramento, CA: Author.

California Postsecondary Education Commission. (2000b). *Enrollment of Hispanics in the U.S., CSU, CCC and private colleges.* Sacramento, CA: Author.

California Postsecondary Education Commission. (2004–05). (http://www.cpec.ca.gov/onlinedata/generatereport/asp).

California Postsecondary Education Commission. (2006). (http://www.cpec.ca.gov/onlinedata/generatereport/asp).

Campaign for College Opportunity. (2005, May 11). *Listen up: Californians respond to the college-access crisis.* Oakland, CA: Author.

Campaign for College Opportunity. (2005, June 22). California can solve shortage of college graduates (http://www.collegecampaign.org/press-room/index.html).

Campaign for College Opportunity. (2006, October 19). College-going rate in California trends down, study finds (http://www.collegecampaign.org/press-room/pressreleases.html).

Campos-Flores, A. (2005, May 30). A Latino power surge. *Newsweek,* pp. 25–35.

Carter, T. P. (1970). *Mexican Americans in school: A history of educational neglect.* New York: College Entrance Examination Board.

Chapa, J., & De La Rosa, B. (2004). "Latino population growth, socioeconomic and demographic characteristics, and implications for educational attainment." *Education and Urban Society, 36*(2), 130–149.

Chicano Coordinating Council on Higher Education. (1969). *El plan de Santa Barbara: A Chicano plan for higher education.* Oakland, CA: La Causa Publications.

Clayton, M. (2003, November 10). College presidents seek to close minority gap. *Christian Science Monitor.*

College Board. (2001). *Annual financial college going rate report.* New York: College Board.

Committee for Economic Development. (2005, May). *Cracks in the education pipeline: A business leader's guide to higher education reform.* Washington, DC: Author.

Cortes, E. (1993). Reweaving the fabric: The iron rule and the IAF strategy for power and politics. In H. G. Cisneros (ed.), *Interwoven destinies* (pp. 294–319). New York: Norton.

Cortés, M. (1999). Do Hispanic nonprofits foster Hispanic philanthropy? In *Hispanic philanthropy: Exploring the factors that influence giving and asking*. New Directions for Philanthropic Fundraising, No. 24. San Francisco: Jossey-Bass.

Crow, M. (2005). The new American university (http://www.asu.edu/president/newamericanuniversity/).

Cruz, R. (2001, May). Role of the National Hispanic University in higher education. National Hispanic University Commencement.

Davis, J. (2005, April). La vida robot: How four underdogs from the mean streets of Phoenix took on the best from M.I.T. in the national underwater BOT championship. *Wired Magazine*, pp. 123–136.

De Los Santos, A. G., Jr., & De Los Santos, G. E. (2003). "Hispanic-serving institutions in the 21st century: Overview, challenges, and opportunities." *Journal of Hispanic Higher Education*, 2(4), 377–391.

DeLuna-Castro, E., & Kluver, L. (2005). *Texas poverty 101*. Austin, TX: The Center for Public Policy Priorities.

Dewey, J. (1964). Traditional versus progressive education. In B. Johnston (ed.), *Issues in education: An anthology of controversy* (pp. 221–226). Boston: Houghton Mifflin.

Di Maria, F. (2006, October 23). Latinos and the American dream—Some still wait. *Hispanic Outlook*.

Dixit, A. K., & Nalebuff, B. J. (1991). *Thinking strategically: The competitive edge in business, politics, and everyday life*. New York: Norton.

Domhoff, G. W. (1978). *The powers that be: Processes of ruling class domination in America*. New York: Random House.

Drucker, P. F. (1999). *Managing challenges for the 21st century.* New York: Harper-Collins.

Eberly, D. E. (1994). *Building a community of citizens: Civil society in the 21st century.* Lanham, MD: University Press of America.

Eckel, P., & Kezar, A. (2003). *Taking the reins: Institutional transformation in American higher education.* Westport, CT: Praeger.

Education Trust. (2006). *Engines of inequity: Diminishing equity in the nation's premier public universities.* Washington, DC: Author.

Educational Testing Service. (2000). *Crossing the great divide in workforce demands.* Princeton, NJ: Author.

Fain, P. (2005, July 11). Competitive pressure is turning research universities into look-alike institutions, economist warns. *Chronicle of Higher Education Online Today's News* (http://chroniclecom/daily/2005/07/2005071103m.htm).

Florida, R. (2005). *The flight of the creative class.* New York: HarperCollins.

Friedman, J. (2005, September 26). Investment firms focusing on Latinos' purchasing power. *Los Angeles Times,* pp. C1, C6.

Friedman, T. L. (2005). *The world is flat: A brief history of the 21st century.* New York: Farrar, Straus and Giroux.

Gandara, P. (1995). *Over the ivy walls: The educational mobility of low-income Chicanos.* Albany: State University of New York Press.

Gandara, P., with Biel, D. (2001, September). *Paving the way to postsecondary education: K–12 intervention programs for underrepresented youth.* Washington, DC: National Postsecondary Education Cooperative.

García, K. (2005, March). Elite educators: These Hispanics are transforming America's colleges. *Hispanic Magazine,* pp. 22–25.

Gates, B. (2005). National Education Summit on High Schools (http://www.gatesfoundation.org/MediaCenter/Speeches/Co-ChairSpeeches/BillgSpeeches/BGSpeechNGA-050226.htm).

Gibson, D. V., Rhi-Perez, P., et al. (2003). *Cameron County/Matamoros at the crossroads: Assets and challenges for accelerated regional and bi-national development.* Brownsville, TX: The Cross Border Institute for Regional Development at the University of Texas at Brownsville, IC^2 at the University of Texas at Austin.

Gilbert, A. (2005, June 16). Minorities make small gains in science jobs (http://news.zdnet.com/2100-9584_22-5749878.html).

Gilder, G. (1989). *Microcosm: The quantum revolution in economics and technology.* New York: Simon Schuster.

Gilroy, M. (2006, October 23). Hispanics showing new migration patterns. *Hispanic Outlook.*

Glenn, D. (2005, June 17). Remedial courses increase chances that under-prepared students will complete their degrees. *Chronicle of Higher Education,* p. 12.

Gloria, A. M., & Castellanos, J. (2003). Latina/o and African American students at predominantly White institutions. In J. Castellanos & L. Jones (eds.), *The majority in the minority.* Sterling, VA: Stylus.

Gonzales, R. (1967). Yo soy Joaquin (http://www.latinamericanstudies.org/latinos/joaquin.htm).

Hall, D. (2005, June). *Getting honest about graduation rates: How states play the numbers and students lose.* Washington, DC: The Education Trust.

Haney Lopez, I. T. (2006, November 3). "How color blindness perpetuates white dominance". *Chronicle of Higher Education,* 11(53), Section B.

Hargroves, K., & Smith,. M. A. (2005). *The natural advantage of nations: Business opportunities, innovations and governance in the 21st century.* Sterling, VA: Earthscan.

Haro, R. P., Rodriguez, G., Jr., & Gonzales, J. L., Jr. (1994, September). *Latino persistence in higher education*. San Francisco: Latino Issues Forum.

Harvard Civil Rights Project. (2005, March). *Confronting the graduation rate crisis in California*. Cambridge, MA: Harvard Civil Rights Project.

Hebel, S. (2006, November). "In rural America, few people harvest 4-year degrees". *Chronicle of Higher Education, 11*(53), p. 20A.

Hernandez, M. (2004a, July 5). Latinos and education in America, *Hispanic Vista* (http://www.hispanicvista.com/html4/071104hernandez.htm).

Hernandez, M. (2004b, May 19). Who speaks and who speaks not for education. *El Tecolote*.

Hispanic Association on Corporate Responsibility. (2004). *Translating economic strength into political power* (http://www.hacr.org/research/pubID.66/pub_detail.asp).

Hispanic Educational Telecommunications Systems. (2005, October). Virtual plaza for student learning and support and the HETS online mentoring program. Presentation at Hispanic Association of Colleges and Universities, San Antonio, Texas.

Hodgkinson, H. (1985). *All one system: Demographics of education— Kindergarten through graduate school*. Washington, DC: Institute for Educational Leadership.

Hodgkinson, H. (1999). *All one system: A second look*. Washington, DC: Institute for Educational Leadership.

Humes, E. (2006, October 26). A GI Bill for the 21st century. *Los Angeles Times*.

Intercultural Development Research Association. (2006, October). *Newsletter, 33*(9).

James, S. D. (2005, June 19). For illegal immigrants, a harsh lesson. *New York Times* (http://www.nytimes.com/2005/06/19/nyregion/19njCOVER.html?

ei=5088&en=a9da743c3044e115&ex=1276833600&partner=rssnyt&emc
=rss&pagewanted=print).

Jaschik, S. (2006, October 30). Minority gains and gaps. *Inside Higher Education*
(http://insidehighered.com/news/2006/10/30/minorities).

Kamman, J. (2005, June 9). 1 in 2 new Americans since 2000 is Hispanic. *Arizona Republic*, p. A1.

Kamman, J. (2006, May 10). Latinos dominate growth in nation. *Arizona Republic*, p. A8.

Kantorwitz, B. (2005, May 16). America's best high schools, ranking in top 100: The testing debate. *Newsweek*.

Katsinas, S., & Palmer, J., et. al. (2004, October 26). *State funding for community colleges: Perceptions from the field.* Norman, IL: Center for the Study of Education Policy, Illinois State University.

W.K. Kellogg Foundation. (2005). *From vision to innovative impact.* Battle Creek, MI: Author.

Kelly, F. (2005, July 22). The westerner. *Chronicle of Higher Education* (http://chronicle.com/free/v51/i46/46a01401.htm).

Kerner, O., & Lindsay, J. (1968). *Report of National Advisory Commission on Civil Disorders.* Washington, DC: U.S. Government Printing Office.

Kochhar, R., Suro, R., & Tafoya, S. (2005). *The new Latino south: The context and consequences of rapid population growth.* Washington, DC: Pew Hispanic Center (http://pewhispanic.org/reports/report.php?ReportID=50).

LaVoo, G. (Producer), & Cardoso, P. (Director). (2002). *Real women have curves.* New York, HBO Films.

Lingenfelter, P. E., & Lenth, C. S. (2005, May/June). What should reauthorization be about? *Change Magazine*, pp. 12–19.

Lopez, E. S. (2002). *The composition of staff in California community colleges, 1994 to 2002*. Sacramento, CA: California Research Bureau, California State Library, pp. 13, 23, 24, 25, 33.

Lopez, E. S., & Rochin, R. I. (2001). *California State University faculty, 1985 to 2001*. Sacramento, CA: California Research Bureau, California State Library, pp. 21–23.

López, R. E., & Samora, J. (1977). George Sánchez and testing. In A. Paredes (ed.), *Humanidad: Essays in honor of George I. Sánchez* (pp. 107–115). Los Angeles: UCLA, Chicano Studies Center Publications.

Madrid, A. (1997, June 4). *Less is not more in the case of education*. Brooklyn College commencement address.

Manzo, K. K., & Cavanna, S. (2005, July 27). South posts big gains in long-term NAEP in reading and math. *Education Week*.

McWilliams, C. (1968). *North from Mexico: The Spanish speaking people in the United States*. New York: Greenwood Press.

Mellando, R., & Yochelson, J. (2006, October 3). Growing Latino technical workforce keeps U.S. competitive. *San Jose Mercury News*.

Mendez v. Westminster School District, Civil Action No. 388 (W.D. Texas, June 1945).

Miller, D. (1979). *Social justice*. Oxford, England: Clarendon Press.

Mills, C. W. (1956). *The power elite*. New York: Oxford University Press.

Mingle, J., Chaloux, B., & Birks, A. (2005). *Investing wisely in adult learning is key to state prosperity*. Atlanta, GA: Southern Regional Education Board.

More residents are earning degrees than in the past, following national trends. (2002, August 19). *San Antonio Express-News*.

Moreno, J. F. (2002, September). "The long term outcomes of Puente." *Educational Policy*, 4(16).

Morin, R. (1966). *Among the valiant: Mexican Americans in WWII and Korea.* Alhambra, CA: Borden.

Murdock, S. (2003). *The new Texas challenge: Population change and the future Texas.* College Station, TX: Texas A&M University.

Murdock, S. (2004, October 24). Comments made during *Update on State Demographics.* Texas Higher Education Coordinating Board, Agenda Item III, Major Policy Action/Discussion.

Murdock, S. (2005, March 18). Listen to the prophet. *Texas Observer.*

National Center for Education Statistics. (2002). *Digest of education statistics,* tables 206 and 207. Washington, DC: Author.

National Center for Higher Education Management Systems. (2005). (http://www.higheredinfo.org/datamaps.php).

National Center for Statistics. (2003). U.S. Census Bureau, 2003 *Population estimates, census 2000,* Table A-5.

National Commission on Excellence in Education. (1983). *A nation at risk.* Washington, DC: U.S. Government Printing Office.

Newman, F. (1985). *Higher education and the American resurgence.* Lawrenceville, NJ: Princeton University Press.

Nora, A. (2003). Access to higher education for Hispanic students: Real or illusory. In J. Castellanos, & L. Jones (eds.), *The majority in the minority.* Sterling, VA: Stylus.

Ohmae, K. (1990). *The borderless world: Power and strategy in the interlinked economy.* New York: Harper Business.

Organization for Economic Cooperation and Development. (2006, November). *Focus on higher education: 2005–06 edition.* Washington, DC: Center for Educational Research and Innovation.

Pew Hispanic Center. (2006a). *Hispanics at mid-decade*. Washington, DC: Author.

Pew Hispanic Center. (2006b, October). *Fact sheet*. Washington, DC: Author.

President's Advisory Commission on Educational Excellence for Hispanic Americans. (1996, September).

Public Policy Institute of California. (1999). *California Count*. San Francisco, CA: Author.

Public Policy Institute of California. (2005, June). *California 2025: It's your choice*. Berkeley: University of California Press.

Robbins, S. P. (2003). *Organizational behavior* (rev. ed.). Upper Saddle River, NJ: Prentice Hall.

Robles, B. (2005). Assets and capacity building opportunities and challenges in Latino community. Presentation at the Annual Conference of National Association for Latino Community Asset Builders. Albuquerque, New Mexico.

Rodriguez v. San Antonio Independent School District. (1973).V. 411 U.S. 1.

Rooke, D., & Torbert, T. R. (2005, April). Seven transformations of leadership. *Harvard Business Review*, pp. 71–72.

Royce, A., & Rodriguez, R. (1996). From personal charity to organized Hispanic institutions and values of stewardship and philanthropy. Unpublished paper, Indiana University Center on Philanthropy.

Santa Ana ENLACE. (2005). *Pathway Project*. Fullerton, CA: California State University, Office of Student Affairs.

Santiago, D. (2005). *Latinos in undergraduate education* (http://www.edexcelencia.org/pdf/Latinos_UG-2004.pdf).

Sarason, S. (1995). *School change: The personal development of a point of view*. New York: Teachers College Press.

Sassen, S. (2005, Winter/Spring). The global city: Introducing a concept. *The Brown Journal of World Affairs, 11*(2). Providence, RI: Brown University.

Schermerhorn, J. R., Jr. (2002). *Management* (7th ed.). Hoboken, NJ: Wiley.

Schevitz, T. (2005, May 2). U.C. System struggles to attract minorities. *San Francisco Chronicle.*

Schmidt, P. (2003, November 28). Academe's Hispanic future: The nation's largest minority group faces obstacles in higher education, and colleges struggle to find the right ways to help. *Chronicle of Higher Education Special Report.*

Spring, J. H. (1976). *The sorting machine: National education policy since 1945.* Mahwah, NJ: Erlbaum.

Stern, E. (2006, September 7). Study: California lagging in key college measures, "report card" shows state trailing U.S. many other nations. *Sacramento Bee.*

Suggs, W. (2005, March 21). Colleges face new demands for accountability, conference speakers say. *Chronicle of Higher Education* (http://chronicle.com/daily/2005/03/2005032101n.htm).

Swail, W. S., Cabrera, A. F., & Lee, C. (2004, June 23). *Latino youth and the pathway to college.* Washington, DC: Pew Hispanic Center.

Tapscott, D. (1996). *The digital economy: Promise and peril in the age of networked intelligence.* New York: McGraw-Hill.

Texas Education Agency. (2005). *Standard school data report for 2005* (http://www.tea.state.tx.us/perfreport/aeis/2005/state.html).

Texas Higher Education Coordinating Board. (2002). *Non-faculty personnel by gender, ethnic origin, executive/administrative/managerial, Texas Public community colleges, Fall 2001.* Austin, TX: Texas Higher Education Coordinating Board, Data and Statistics.

Texas Higher Education Coordinating Board. (2004a). *Tenured faculty headcount by gender, ethnic origin: Texas public universities, Fall 2003.* Austin, TX: Texas Higher Education Coordinating Board, Data and Statistics.

Texas Higher Education Coordinating Board. (2004b, June). *The Texas higher education plan: Closing the gaps by 2015: Annual performance review.* Austin, TX: Texas Higher Education Coordinating Board, Data and Statistics.

Time Magazine. (2006, April 11). The dropout nation.

Tinto, V. (2004, July). Student retention and graduation: Facing the truth, living with the consequences. The Pell Institute (http://www.pellinstitute.org/ tinto/tintoOccasionalPaperRetention.pdf).

Tomas Rivera Policy Brief. (2003, April). Los Angeles: Tomas Rivera Policy Institute (http://www.trpi.org).

Tornatzky, L. G., et al. (2002, April). *College knowledge: What Latino parents need to know and why they don't know it.* Los Angeles: Tomas Rivera Policy Institute.

U.S. Census Bureau. (1996). Projects of the Top 10 States, Ranked by Population Size: 1995–2025. PPL-47 (http://www.census.gov/population/www/ projections/ppl47.html).

U.S. Census Bureau. (2000). *Education participation by race and ethnicity.* Washington, DC: Department of Commerce.

U.S. Census Bureau. (2002, March). *Hispanic population in the U.S.* (P 20–545). Washington, DC: Department of Commerce.

U.S. Census Bureau. (2003). Education and school enrollment (http:// www.census.gov/population/www/cen2000/phc-t39.html).

U.S. Census Bureau. (2004). 2050 projection (http://www.census.gov/prod/ 2004pubs/p 20–550.pdf).

U.S. Census Bureau. (2005, January 19). *Population estimates data sets and people data profiles and rankings of median age.* Washington, DC: Government Printing Office.

United States Hispanic Chamber of Commerce. (n.d.). Statistics: Population & Economic Strength (http://www.ushcc.com/res-statistics.html).

U.S. Department of Education. (2004). *National Center for Education Statistics, 2002-03.* Integrated Data System (IPEDS). Table 263.

U.S. Department of Education. Federal TRIO programs (http://www.ed.gov/about/offices/list/ope/trio/index.html).

University of California. (2003, March). *California's future: It starts here, UC's contributions to economic growth, health and culture.* Section 5, pp. 5–9.

Valverde, L. A. (ed.). (2002, March). *A compromised commitment: Society's obligation and failure to serve the nation's largest growing population.* Tempe, AZ: The Hispanic Border Leadership Institute, Arizona State University.

Valverde, L. A. (2006). *Improving schools for Latinos: Creating better learning environments.* Lanham, MD: Rowan and Littlefield Education.

Varsalona, D. (2005, July 27). Hispanic population soars in the southeast. *Chronicle of Higher Education.*

Vernez, G., & Mizell, L. (2001). *Goal: To double the rate of Hispanics earning a bachelor's degree.* Santa Monica, CA: RAND/Education.

Wagner, L., & Derek, A. F. (eds.). (1999, Summer). *Hispanic philanthropy: Exploring the factors that influence giving and asking.* New Directions for Philanthropic Fundraising, No. 24. San Francisco: Jossey-Bass.

Warren, M. (2005, Summer). "Communities and schools: A new view of urban education reform." *Harvard Educational Review, 75*(2).

Washburn, J. (2004, January/February). The tuition crunch: For low income students college is increasingly out of reach. *Atlantic Monthly.*

Welch, J., & Welch, S. (2005). *Winning.* New York: Harper Business.

Western Interstate Commission for Higher Education (WICHE). (2005). *Knocking at the door: Projections of high school graduates by state, income, and race/ethnicity.* Boulder, CO: Author

Wheary, J. (2005, May 17). Support the future of immigrant students (http://newswire.ascribe.org/cgi-bin/behold.pl?ascribeid+20050517.095152time+11%20PDT&public=0).

Wolfson, J. (2005, May). University, Inc. *Boston Magazine*.

Yosso, T. J., & Solorzano, D. G. (2006, March). *Leaks in the Chicana and Chicano educational pipeline*. Latino Policy & Issues Brief no. 13. Los Angeles, CA: UCLA Chicano Studies Research Center.

Zuniga, V., & Hernandez-Leon, R. (2005). *New destinations: Mexican immigration in the United States*. New York: Russell Sage Foundation.

Index

LULAC. *See* League of United Latin American Citizens (LULAC)
Lumina Foundation for Education, 216

M

Madrid, A., 71–72
Maidique, M., 210
MALDEF. *See* Mexican American Legal Defense and Educational Fund (MALDEF),
Manufacturing jobs, 117
Manzo, K. K., 40
Marianist missionaries, 43
Marshall Plan, 155
Martí, J., 202
Mass education, 175
Master's degrees, 65
Mathematics: access and retention strategies for, 84; educational preparation for, 173; K–12 initiatives for, 54–55; lack of Latinos in, 60; mentoring in, 174–175; outreach programs for, 187–188
Mathematics, Engineering, and Science Achievement (MESA) program, 84, 187–188
Matute, A. M., 202
McDonald's Corporation, 195
McGrath, P., 185
McNair Program, 91
McWilliams, C., 4
Medicaid, 112–113
Melendez v. Westminster School District, 44
Mellando, R., 156
Mentoring: in math and sciences, 174–175; and philanthropy strategies, 38; in Puente Project, 185–186; in retention programs, 88, 90
Merit scholarships, 171
MESA. *See* Mathematics, Engineering, Science Achievement (MESA) program

Mexican American Legal Defense and Educational Fund (MALDEF), 36, 94, 128
Mexican American School Board Members Association, 94
Mexican American Youth Association, 79
Mexican American Youth Organization, 79
Mexican Americans: achievements of, 4; community citizenship of, 141–144; and diversity of Hispanic community, 126; economic participation of, 140–141; educational development of, 137–140; historical roots of, 126–128; and leadership for sustainability, 131–136; social status of, 6; technology literacy of, 144–145; visioning and planning of, 136–137
Mexican Americans in School: A History of Educational Neglect (Carter), 6
Mexico, 115, 120, 133–134
Middle-class Latinos, 20
Middle-class society, 157–158, 171
Miller, D., 127–128
Mills, C. W., 183–184
Mingle, J., 12
Mistral, G., 202
Mizell, L., 172
Money transfers, 12–13
Montoya, J., 4
Moreno, J. F., 186
Morin, R., 4
Motivation, 147
Movimiento Estudiantil Chicano de Aztlán, 79
Murdock, S., 7, 42, 64

N

NAFTA. *See* North American Free Trade Agreement (NAFTA)
Nalebuff, B. J., 137
National Assessment of Educational Progress, 13–14, 40